In the Mood for Food

For Phil, my rock

MICHAEL JOSEPH

Published by the Penguin Group
Penguin Books Ltd, 80 Strand, London
WC2R 0RL, England
Penguin Group (USA) Inc., 375 Hudson Street, New York,
New York 10014, USA
Penguin Group (Canada), 90 Eglinton Avenue East,
Suite 700, Toronto, Ontario, Canada M4P 2Y3
(a division of Pearson Penguin Canada Inc.)
Penguin Ireland, 25 St Stephen's Green, Dublin 2, Ireland
(a division of Penguin Books Ltd)
Penguin Group (Australia), 250 Camberwell Road,
Camberwell, Victoria 3124, Australia
(a division of Pearson Australia Group Pty Ltd)
Penguin Books India Pvt Ltd, 11 Community Centre,
Panchsheel Park, New Delhi – 110 017, India
Penguin Group (NZ), 67 Apollo Drive, Mairangi Bay,
Auckland 1310, New Zealand
(a division of Pearson New Zealand Ltd)
Penguin Books (South Africa) (Pty) Ltd,
24 Sturdee Avenue, Rosebank, Johannesburg 2196,
South Africa

Penguin Books Ltd, Registered Offices: 80 Strand,
London WC2R 0RL, England

www.penguin.com

First published 2007
1

Copyright © Jo Pratt, 2007
Illustrations by Yeti McCaldin,
Copyright © Yeti McCaldin, 2007
All photography by Gus Filgate unless otherwise stated
Copyright © Gus Filgate, 2007
Jacket photograph by Chris Terry, also photography on
pages 7, 52 (centre), 171, 190 (bottom centre), 192, 217,
242 (centre)
Copyright © Chris Terry, 2007

The moral right of the author has been asserted

With thanks to the following for their kind contributions:

Typhoon International for supplying kitchenware for use in
the photographs. For product information, mail order and
store details visit *www.typhooneurope.com*

Ethos for supplying kitchenware for use in the photographs.
For product information, mail order and store details visit
www.ethoshousewares.com

Paperchase for supplying art papers for use throughout this
book. For product information, mail order and store details
visit *www.paperchase.co.uk*

Orla Kiely for supplying fabric for use in the design of this
book (page 80–81). For local stockists, mail order and
online store visit *www.orlakiely.com*

Set in Mrs Eaves

Printed in Great Britain by Butler & Tanner Ltd, Frome,
Somerset

A CIP catalogue record for this book is available from
the British Library

ISBN: 978–0–718–14858–4

In the Mood for Food

Jo Pratt

Michael Joseph

an imprint of Penguin Books

Contents

Introduction

I've been eating, sleeping and living food since I started writing this book — not that I ever had food out of my mind for long before then. I wake up in the morning thinking about what to cook for dinner. Once I've finished eating one meal, I'm wondering about the next. Some of my first childhood memories are based around cooking, so when the time came for me to choose a career route, I followed my heart (or was it my stomach?) and I have since worked with Michelin-starred chefs, written recipes for magazines such as *Elle* and *Olive*, and appeared on various television programmes. But when it boils down to it, I'm a home cook and what I enjoy making is fabulous-tasting, great-looking food that's fuss and stress free.

What I cook at home depends hugely on what sort of mood I'm in. One day I might be feeling wonderfully extravagant and want to prepare a glamorous dinner for my husband Phil and some friends. Another day I'll be in a really lazy mood and can't be bothered to spend long cooking at all. Our moods can change as quickly as the weather and it is amazing how they dictate our day and what we fancy eating. I bet there are loads of times when you've planned a meal in advance and when it comes to cooking or eating it, you've gone off the idea. It's the same sort of thing when we go out to a restaurant. One time you might fancy, say, bangers and mash because you feel in need of some comfort. Another time when you go to the same place, you order a big salad because your mood is telling you to be a little healthier and good to yourself. If it's our moods that influence what we want to eat, then it's certainly worth taking care of them and making sure we pamper them with delicious food.

So this is where this book comes in. I've taken what I consider to be six influential moods and given each their own chapter:

In the Mood for Being Healthy This is when we want to be pure and eat light, well-balanced foods that make us feel full of vitality and have that fantastic feel-good factor.

In the Mood for Something Naughty but Nice Oh dear, the evil mood, when we crave naughty addictive foods that are chocolaty, sugary, creamy . . . basically anything that's bad for you.

In the Mood for Some Comfort The foods that we turn to in times of stress, when we've had one too many, we don't feel well or when the days are dark and miserable. Food whose soothing nature gives us temporary relief.

In the Mood for Being Lazy For those times when you can't be bothered to do much cooking, but still want to eat something really tasty and satisfying.

In the Mood for Being Extravagant Fabulous occasions when you want to really go to town and be totally glam. It's a chance to show off, be lavish and treat everyone, and yourself, to exceptional food and drink.

In the Mood for Being Romantic When we put all of our thoughts and time into each other, show how we feel with our cooking and enhance our mood with aphrodisiac foods.

All the recipes are for real people making real food and you'll be pleased to know that they are easy to follow. There's a rough guide to the cooking times to make life less of a rush and I've used time-saving ingredients where possible (what's wrong with the odd ready-made ingredient from time to time?). I've included a PS at the end of many recipes to highlight any shortcuts, tips or alternative ingredient suggestions that I could think of. You'll also find a couple of dinner party menus and plenty of great drink suggestions.

So forget slaving in the kitchen for hours on end, getting in a sweat over a technique you don't even know how to pronounce, let alone perform, or hunting high and low for ingredients you haven't even heard of. Let's be realistic — we have busy lives to lead, but if you love eating good food, then I'm sure you'll love all these straightforward recipes. Whatever mood you're in, just turn the pages to find that edible solution.

Enjoy!

x

In the Mood for Being
Healthy

If I find I'm in the mood for being healthy, then it's all about wanting to be pure and good to myself when it comes to eating. Forget fancy diets here. To me it's not about losing weight, but more about tucking into light, well-balanced foods that make me feel full of vitality. The recipes here will show you that it doesn't have to be hard to make great-tasting meals, full of essential nutrients and low in fat, without going overboard on the carbs.

The mood for being healthy hits me for all sorts of reasons. Monday mornings are a classic example. After a weekend of eating out a lot, watching films and not doing enough exercise, I wake up on Monday (wishing it was still the weekend) with good intentions to have a healthy day. Fruit smoothies and nutritious cereals are the best way to begin the week and if I've started off healthy, it's more likely to continue through the rest of the day. So the health experts are right: breakfast really is the most important meal of the day.

If the healthy mood falls over a weekend, you need more substantial brunch recipes that are full of energy-giving ingredients, low in fat, but full of flavour. Foods that won't make you want to go back to bed to sleep them off. What you need is a breakfast that makes you rise and then shine all day.

Now, working-day lunchtimes can be a challenge. I regularly find myself in the mood for a healthy lunch when I know I've a busy afternoon ahead and want to be alert or if I'm planning on wearing something special that night and don't want to have a bloated tummy. The problem, though, is finding something healthy to eat other than a soggy, shop-bought 'healthy' sandwich or a salad laced with mayonnaise or an oily dressing. But with just a little planning and preparation, fresh, home-made salads are a healthy, tasty solution.

At the beginning of the summer, when you know that there aren't going to be so many layers of clothes to hide under and there's a beach holiday looming (yikes), you can often find you're suddenly in the mood for healthy food. Or perhaps in January when, after total indulgence through the festive period, you hit the supermarkets, loading your basket with stacks of healthy-looking foods. Alternatively, you may quite simply be having one of those 'fat days', and no matter which way you turn, your bum looks big.

But what about when you want to entertain and have friends round for a dinner party? If it clashes with your mood for eating healthily, it can seem like a major nightmare. It's not that you mind your friends knowing you're choosing healthy options, that's certainly nothing to be ashamed about, but you don't want to make a song and dance about the fact that it took you five minutes longer than usual to squeeze into your jeans before they arrived. If you're lacking inspiration for great-tasting meals with that feel-good factor, then there are certainly plenty of ideas in this chapter for you.

Rise and Shine
Healthy breakfasts for the perfect start

I wish I could jump out of bed, especially on bright, sunny mornings, but I rarely can. However, once I'm up, seeing the sun shining often puts me in the mood for a healthy breakfast (unless I'm hungover, when I need the kind of comfort food you'll find on page 101). Eating a healthy breakfast is the best way to give your energy levels a boost. You'll be more alert and, even better, you are more likely to be in the mood for healthy food all day. Forget the fry-up and high-sugar cereals; if you are in the mood for being healthy, think fresh fruit and vegetables, bio-live yoghurts, wholegrains, eggs, nuts and seeds. It's amazing how easily you can create supertasty light foods to start your day.

The thing is though, weekdays are a challenge for most of us. It's when I'm racing about, trying to get out of the door on time, that my blender comes in handy for making smoothies and juices. And all those essential nutrients are a brilliant way to give your body a kick-start. If, however, it's cold outside or a smoothie isn't what you are in the mood for, you could have a go at making blueberry and apple porridge. All you need to do is simmer one part oats in two parts water or milk until creamy. I use semi-skimmed milk rather than water so I can get a good dose of calcium. Add a handful of blueberries and half or one grated apple and heat until the blueberries are starting to burst. The natural sugars from the fruit may well be enough for you, but if you prefer your porridge to be sweeter, add a little honey.

Weekends are a different matter. There is more time to spend over breakfast, depending how lazy you're feeling. It's the best time of day to relax and have a leisurely bite to eat. Energy food is usually what I'm after: things that are low in fat, high in goodness and full of flavour. Foods that won't make me want to go straight back to bed to sleep them off.

Breakfast Berry Smoothie

The best thing about whipping up this smoothie is that if you're in a rush (and let's face it, most of us are in the mornings) it's like having your whole breakfast in a glass. The addition of wheatgerm and yoghurt will fill you up far more than a smoothie made just from fruit.

* **makes two large, superhealthy glasses**
   takes about 5 minutes to make

Place everything in a blender and blitz well until there are no lumps. If it seems too thick, just add some more pomegranate or cranberry juice. The sweetness of berries varies, so if the smoothie isn't sweet enough for your taste, blend in a little maple syrup or runny honey. Pour into two large glasses and enjoy straight away.

250ml chilled pomegranate
   or cranberry juice
1 banana, roughly chopped
100g fresh or frozen raspberries
100g blueberries
1 small pot of plain or fruit
   low-fat bio-live yoghurt
2–3 tablespoons wheatgerm

PS... *If you are not keen on the little seeds from raspberries, then blitz the raspberries first with the blueberries and pomegranate or cranberry juice and strain through a sieve. Place back in the blender and blitz with the banana, yoghurt and wheatgerm.*

You don't have to stick to the fruits I have suggested – why not try strawberries, blackberries, blackcurrants or stoned cherries. If fresh berries are out of season, then grab a bag of frozen mixed berries instead.

Tropical Fruit Smoothie

Bring some sunshine to the start of your day with a smoothie made entirely from tropical fruit (see picture on page 15). After a glass of this you'll feel full of get-up-and-go because it's packed with vitamin C. The enzymes from the pineapple are great for your digestion, which maximizes the extraction of all of the other nutrients in the drink and will give a huge boost to your energy levels. Shut your eyes, take a long sip and dream of being somewhere hot, sunny and tropical.

*** makes two generous glasses
   takes about 10 minutes to make**

Scoop out the pulp from the passion fruit into a blender. This can be strained through a sieve if you don't want the seeds. Add the remaining ingredients and blitz until you have a smooth consistency. Pour into glasses and enjoy straight away.

2 passion fruit

**1 ripe mango,
   peeled and chopped**

**1 small pineapple,
   peeled and cut into chunks**

**10–14 canned or fresh lychees,
   peeled and stoned**

juice of ½ lime

about 8–10 ice cubes

PS . . . *Fresh fruits vary hugely as to how much juice they contain. If the smoothie is too thick for you, then add a splash of fresh orange, pineapple or apple juice.*

If you want to transform this from a juice drink to more of a breakfast in a glass, then add a banana and a low-fat bio-live yoghurt to the blender with a splash of orange, pineapple or apple juice rather than the ice.

Supervitality Juice

This delicious combination of ingredients creates a real power juice, which will leave you feeling full of vitality. Apples and pears are brilliant for helping the body break down cholesterol, kiwi fruit are energy enhancing and the celery can keep blood pressure low. Wow, what a great drink to wake up to. You will need a juicer to make this, but as it is quite possibly the healthiest bit of electrical kitchen kit you can have, it will be well worth the money.

* makes one large glass
takes about 5 minutes to make

Wash all of the ingredients and cut them into a suitable size to fit into the juicer. To extract the maximum amount of goodness, don't peel them first.

Switch the machine on and push everything through. As soon as the juice comes out, the clear liquid will sit at the bottom and a vibrant green froth will rise to the surface. Drink it all straight away, stirring with a straw as you go.

1 apple
1 ripe pear
1 kiwi fruit
1 stick of celery
1 small knob of fresh ginger

Herby Egg White Omelette with Vine Tomatoes and Crispy Parma Ham

An egg white omelette may not sound that appealing, but believe me, this one tastes great and is remarkably healthy. This is a fantastic light brunch, one that is high in protein from the egg white, lower in fat by not using the egg yolk and carb-free, so it won't make you feel tired or bloated afterwards.

* **makes one omelette, but you can easily increase quantities to make more**

  takes about 15 minutes to make

Preheat the grill to medium/high.

Place the tomatoes and Parma ham on a baking tray, season with pepper and sprinkle a little olive oil and then the Parmesan over the tomatoes.

Place under the grill for 3 to 4 minutes, turning the Parma ham halfway through so it goes really nice and crispy. If the Parma ham cooks before the tomatoes, just remove from the tray and keep warm. The tomatoes are done when their skins are just starting to burst open. If they need a little longer, make sure you keep your eye on them, as they will become mushy if left too long.

Brush a little olive oil in a small (15 to 18cm) non-stick frying pan and place over a medium heat.

Lightly whisk together the egg whites, herbs and a good pinch of celery salt. Pour into the pan and continuously stir around with a rubber spatula until the eggs are setting like scrambled egg, and then leave to continue cooking until the whites are cooked through and not runny.

Carefully fold over, transfer the omelette to a warm plate and serve with the juicy tomatoes and crispy Parma ham.

6 cherry tomatoes (on the vine if possible, but not the end of the world if they're not)

2–3 slices of Parma ham

freshly ground black pepper

olive oil

½–1 tablespoon finely grated Parmesan cheese

3 egg whites

1–2 tablespoons chopped herbs (choose a selection of whatever you fancy, such as basil, chives, chervil, parsley, tarragon, oregano or dill, but stick to the nice soft-leaf herbs, rather than coarse ones such as rosemary or thyme)

celery salt

Roast Mushrooms and Poached Eggs on Toast with Raw Energy Salsa

This is true energy food and makes a really nutritionally balanced breakfast or brunch. Serving the salsa raw is the best way to get a high level of pure nutrients from the peppers and tomatoes and the vitamin E and B6-rich avocado is great for a quick-acting nervous system. If you can, make the salsa just before you need it because once the peppers and tomatoes are cut, they start to lose some of their fantastic goodness.

* **serves two**
  takes about 20 minutes to make

Preheat the oven to 180°C/fan 160°C/gas 4.

Make the salsa first by mixing everything together and seasoning with salt and pepper.

Place the mushrooms in a roasting tray and brush with a little olive oil. Season with salt and pepper and roast for 8 to 10 minutes until they are golden and tender.

While the mushrooms are cooking, bring a pan of water to a simmer with the vinegar. Crack the eggs individually into cups, and then add one egg at a time into the water. Once the water has returned to a simmer, poach the eggs for 3 minutes. Lift out with a slotted spoon and sit on kitchen paper to remove the excess water.

Place the roasted mushrooms on the toasted bread (drizzled with a little extra-virgin olive oil if you like) and top with the poached eggs. Spoon on the salsa and serve.

PS . . . *For the best poached eggs, make sure they are as fresh as possible.*

In the mood for a drink? *For a refreshing juice, blitz some freshly squeezed orange juice (store your oranges in the fridge for chilled juice) in a blender with a small handful of mint leaves.*

for the salsa

½ **red pepper, finely chopped**

½ **green pepper, finely chopped**

2 **ripe tomatoes, deseeded and finely chopped**

½ **ripe avocado, chopped**

1 **tablespoon chopped parsley**

¼ **teaspoon red wine vinegar**

1 **tablespoon extra-virgin olive oil**

sea salt and freshly ground black pepper

for the mushrooms and eggs on toast

4 **large flat mushrooms**

olive oil

sea salt and freshly ground black pepper

4 **tablespoons white wine or malt vinegar**

2–4 **really fresh eggs (depending on how hungry you are)**

2–4 **slices of toasted grainy, wholemeal or nutty bread (the sort that looks like it is full of healthy flavour)**

Banana and Walnut Pancakes with Pineapple Syrup

This is definitely one for the weekend. Put the coffee on, squeeze some fresh juice and whip up these tasty American-style pancakes, made from high-fibre wholemeal flour and energy-giving banana. The syrup can be made in advance and kept in the fridge, but if you are pushed for time, then a drizzle of maple syrup over the pancakes also works a treat. For a less sweet option, spoon over some ripe passion fruit.

* **makes about ten pancakes, serving two to four**
  takes about 20 to 25 minutes to make

First of all, you need to make the syrup, which can be made well in advance and kept in the fridge for a couple of weeks. Boil together the pineapple juice, sugar and lime juice for 6 to 8 minutes or until just half the liquid is left, creating a syrup-like consistency. Remove from the heat and leave to cool.

To make the pancakes, mix together the flour, baking powder, mixed spice, caster sugar, walnuts and sultanas. Add the egg and milk, stirring quickly to form a batter.

Heat a frying pan over a medium heat and brush with just a little sunflower oil. Drop three or four individual tablespoons of the batter into the pan, depending on how many you can fit without them joining together, and cook for 1 minute. Top each pancake with a couple of slices of banana and cook until bubbles appear on the surface. Turn over the pancakes and cook for a further 2 minutes until they are golden.

Keep the pancakes warm while you cook the rest (if you can resist eating them straight away), and then serve drizzled with the pineapple syrup and topped with a dollop of Greek yoghurt.

for the syrup
150ml pineapple juice
75g soft brown sugar
1 tablespoon lime juice

for the pancakes
100g wholemeal flour
1 teaspoon baking powder
½ teaspoon mixed spice
1 tablespoon caster sugar
50g chopped walnuts
40g sultanas
1 large egg, beaten
125ml semi-skimmed milk
sunflower oil
1 large or 2 small bananas, sliced
low-fat Greek yoghurt (if you fancy it, but it's not essential)

Cranberry and Orange Breakfast Muffins

These freshly baked muffins are packed full of healthy ingredients, so you won't feel bad if you have more than one. The wholemeal flour gives a huge boost of fibre, and linseeds add omega-3 (great for treating high blood pressure and cholesterol, not to mention boosting your brain power). And it doesn't stop there. The sunflower and pumpkin seeds contain minerals and protein, cranberries and the orange add vitamin C and you even get some calcium from the yoghurt.

* **makes nine muffins**
  takes about 20 to 25 minutes to make

Preheat the oven to 190°C/fan 170°C/gas 5.

Place nine large muffin cases in a deep muffin tin.

Stir together the flour, baking powder, wheatbran, linseed, sunflower and/or pumpkin seeds, sugar, orange zest and cranberries. Add the oil, eggs and yoghurt and mix until just combined. Spoon into the muffin cases and scatter a few oats over each one.

Bake for 25 minutes or until the muffins have risen and are cracking slightly on their tops. Remove from the oven and cool slightly before eating warm.

To eat later, leave the muffins until cool and store in an airtight container for up to a couple of days. You can also freeze the muffins, and then defrost overnight and heat through in a low oven before eating.

175g wholemeal self-raising flour

2 teaspoons baking powder

5 tablespoons wheatbran

2 tablespoons linseed

3 tablespoons sunflower and/or pumpkin seeds

75g soft brown sugar

finely grated zest of 1 large orange

75g dried cranberries

3 tablespoons sunflower oil

2 large eggs

250ml low-fat natural yoghurt

1 tablespoon rolled oats

PS . . . *Instead of cranberries, try sultanas, raisins, dried blueberries or dried cherries.*

In the mood for a drink? *Freshly squeezed orange juice mixed with a little cranberry juice.*

Not a Soggy Sarnie in Sight
Light salads for your lunch break

Eating a healthy lunch can be a challenge. You're starving hungry, yet unable to face another shop-bought, rather unhealthy soggy sarnie. Everything seems to look the same, taste the same, not to mention costs a small fortune. So you decide to look at the salad selection. A salad has to be healthy...right? Wrong! So many bought salads contain loads of mayonnaise or have dressings that are high in fat, salt and additives.

So with that in mind, I have decided to share some of my favourite lunchtime bites for when I'm in the mood for being healthy. They pack neatly into a lunchbox (and boy can you get some funky-looking ones now) to eat at your desk, in the park or on the go. I love these recipes: firstly because they taste so delicious and secondly because they are packed full of fresh, natural ingredients that are usually lower in carbs and fat than bought salads. Finally, I know that I won't be falling asleep in the afternoon in the way you can after eating an overprocessed lunch.

The best thing about these recipes is that most can be prepared the night before without going limp and soggy. Others can be made in no time at all before you head off to work, taking any dressing separately to add at the last minute. If you work from home like I often do, you can simply make up the salad as and when you are in the mood for lunch (even if it is 11 am).

If you find yourself in the mood for a sarnie or worried you won't have time to make a salad beforehand, then rather than making up your sandwich at home before you go to work, take all of the ingredients in little pots or sealable sandwich bags and put them together when you need lunch. My healthy favourite is grainy brown bread filled with lean ham, a handful of watercress and a dollop of low-fat crème fraîche and wholegrain mustard (mixed together and kept in a little plastic pot). It's very tasty, especially with a few cherry tomatoes on the side. You see, not a soggy sarnie in sight.

Tuna, Cannellini and Lemon Salad

The great thing about this salad is that it is wonderfully quick to throw together and uses storecupboard items that seem to come to life when combined with some simple, fresh ingredients. Any beans can be used and all are great for a good dose of low-fat protein and fibre, but I really like the creaminess of cannellini beans.

* **serves two**
  takes about 10 minutes to make

Mix together the tuna, beans, lemon zest, olives, capers, tomatoes, cucumber, parsley and rocket, if you are using it.

Pour the lemon juice, mustard, olive oil and seasoning into a little jar or bottle. Shake well. The dressing is now ready to pour over your salad when you want to eat it.

for the salad

200g tin of tuna in olive oil, drained and flaked

400g tin of cannellini beans, drained

grated zest of 1 lemon

a small handful of juicy black olives, stoned

2 tablespoons capers

8–10 sunblush tomatoes or halved cherry tomatoes

¼ cucumber, chopped or thickly sliced

a large handful of flat-leaf parsley leaves, roughly chopped

a large handful of wild rocket leaves (optional)

for the dressing

1 tablespoon lemon juice

1 teaspoon Dijon mustard

3 tablespoons extra-virgin olive oil

sea salt and freshly ground black pepper

PS . . . *Transform this lunchbox salad into a smart lunch/dinner by making the salad as above, but instead of using tinned tuna, sear or pan-fry some fresh tuna steaks for a minute or so on each side.*

Bulgur Wheat Salad with Feta, Pomegranate and Lots of Herbs

I just can't get enough of this salad. Usually something you love eating so much is bad for you (like chips and crisps), but this is really quite healthy. It's full of fibre from the bulgur wheat; the feta is much lower in fat than most other cheeses; and it has lots of valuable nutrients from the rest of the ingredients.

* serves two
takes about 20 minutes to make

Cook the bulgur wheat according to the packet instructions, and then rinse under the cold tap to cool it down. Drain it really well, shaking in the sieve to separate all the grains, and then tip into a large mixing bowl.

Add the feta, pomegranate seeds, herbs, tomato, spring onion, olive oil and lemon juice. Season with just a little salt (the feta cheese will add a salty flavour) and a good twist of black pepper. Toss together until everything is combined and either serve straight away or keep in the fridge overnight.

100g bulgur wheat

125g feta cheese, finely crumbled

seeds from ½ pomegranate

1 large handful of mint leaves, roughly chopped

1 large handful of flat-leaf parsley, roughly chopped

2 ripe tomatoes, deseeded and chopped

½ bunch spring onions, finely sliced

2 tablespoons extra-virgin olive oil

2 tablespoons lemon juice

sea salt and freshly ground black pepper

PS . . . *The flavours work really well with couscous rather than bulgur wheat, which also makes the recipe even quicker to prepare.*

Prawn, Almond and Basmati Rice Salad

If I have a busy day ahead and plans to go out drinking after work, then I know the balance of low-fat protein in the prawns and good carbohydrates from the rice in this salad will see me through from lunch until late on. Basmati has a lower GI than standard long-grain rice, so you should stay fuller for longer and not be tempted to order a packet of crisps as soon as you get to the bar. The salad is really easy to make, but cook the rice the night before if you're leaving to go to work early in the morning.

✽ serves two generously
   takes about 20 minutes to make

Place the rice in a sieve and rinse it really well under the cold tap for a couple of minutes. Tip it into a saucepan and pour over 200ml water. Add the sultanas and a pinch of salt and bring to the boil. As soon as it is boiling, turn down the heat, cover with a tight-fitting lid and cook for 10 minutes, keeping the lid on throughout. After the 10 minutes is up, remove the pan from the heat and leave it for 5 to 10 minutes without removing the lid at all.

While the rice is cooking, heat a small frying pan and gently toast the flaked almonds and cumin seeds until the almonds are golden.

Fluff up the cooked rice with a fork and tip into a large bowl to cool down. Once the rice is cold, stir in the prawns, carrot, coriander, red onion, toasted almonds and cumin seeds.

In a small bowl, stir together the lemon juice, sugar, olive oil and seasoning until the sugar has dissolved. Pour over the salad and mix well.

for the salad

150g basmati rice

50g sultanas

a pinch of salt

50g flaked almonds

1½ teaspoons cumin seeds

150–200g cooked king prawns

2 carrots, peeled and coarsely grated or very finely shredded

1 small bunch of coriander leaves, roughly chopped

1 small red onion, finely sliced

for the dressing

juice of ½ lemon

1 teaspoon soft light brown sugar

2 tablespoons olive oil

sea salt and freshly ground black pepper

PS . . . *To transform this rice salad into a more substantial dinner, prepare it as above but without the prawns and serve it with: ✽ Skewers of cubed halloumi cheese, courgette and aubergine drizzled with olive oil and grilled or barbecued until golden. ✽ Chicken breast or raw tiger prawns marinated in natural yoghurt, garlic and garam masala, and then grilled or barbecued until cooked through. ✽ Lamb steaks marinated in a little mint sauce and crushed garlic, and then grilled and served with a dollop of natural yoghurt or sour cream.*

Mediterranean Vegetable Couscous

Here's another recipe to make the night before — and this doesn't have to be a chore. Couscous is one of those ingredients that require no effort whatsoever, and while you're preparing your dinner in the evening, just cut up the veggies and let them roast in the oven.

* serves two

takes about 35 minutes to make, including roasting time

Preheat the oven to 200°C/fan 180°C/gas 6.

Cut the red pepper, courgettes, aubergine and red onions into 3 to 4cm pieces and toss in a roasting tray with a tablespoon of the olive oil. Season with salt and pepper and roast for about 25 minutes, turning a couple of times. Add the cherry tomatoes and return to the oven for a further 10 minutes. Remove the vegetables from the oven and leave to cool.

Place the couscous in a large bowl and pour over 350ml boiling water. Briefly stir, cover with a lid or clingfilm and leave for 10 minutes for the water to be absorbed. Fluff up with a fork and leave to cool.

Mix together the remaining tablespoon of olive oil with the pesto and balsamic vinegar. Add this pesto dressing to the roasted vegetables, olives and basil or rocket, if you are using them. Toss everything together with the couscous and eat straight away or store in the fridge for the next day.

1 small red pepper

1 large or 2 small courgettes

1 small aubergine

2 red onions

2 tablespoons extra-virgin olive oil

sea salt and freshly ground black pepper

about 20 cherry tomatoes

200g couscous

1½ tablespoons green pesto

1–2 teaspoons balsamic vinegar (see PS...)

a handful of stoned black olives

a few torn basil leaves or a good handful of rocket leaves (optional)

PS . . . *Some balsamic vinegars are quite sharp. If yours is, then 1 teaspoon should be plenty in the dressing, but if it has a sweeter, mellower flavour, then 2 teaspoons is best.*

Shavings of Parmesan, toasted pine nuts, cooked chicken or strips of cured ham are all really nice additions to this salad.

Vietnamese Chicken Noodle Salad

Lots of crunchy fresh vegetables, juicy shredded chicken and rice noodles tossed together with a lime and chilli dressing make a megahealthy, refreshing lunch. The tangy dressing is fat-free and the veggies certainly give you a generous boost towards your five-a-day. Pack up the salad in a box and tuck into it with chopsticks if you want to be really authentic (or use pencils if you're eating at your desk!).

*** serves two
takes about 20 to 25 minutes to make**

Bring the water or chicken stock to the boil. Add the chicken, cover with a lid and simmer for 5 minutes. Lift out the chicken with a slotted spoon and leave to cool.

Return the liquid to the boil, turn off the heat and add the noodles. Leave to soak for about 4 minutes or until tender, and then drain. Cool under the cold tap and place in a mixing bowl.

Shred the chicken and add to the noodles with the Chinese cabbage, carrot, cucumber, spring onion and herbs.

Mix together all the dressing ingredients until the sugar has dissolved and pour over the salad. Toss the salad and scatter over the peanuts.

PS . . . *If you can't get hold of roasted unsalted peanuts, buy raw shelled peanuts with reddish brown skins on. Roast in a hot, dry frying pan for 2 to 3 minutes until they start to colour. Reduce the heat and continue to roast for a further 5 minutes, tossing them in the pan. Tip on to kitchen paper and rub away their skins.*

In the mood for a drink? *This is delicious with the Ginger and Lime Cordial on page 32.*

for the salad

500ml water or chicken stock

2 skinless chicken breasts

125g thin rice noodles

¼ Chinese leaf/cabbage, finely shredded

I carrot, peeled and cut into matchsticks

¼ cucumber, cut into matchsticks

4 spring onions, sliced into thin strips

a small handful of coriander leaves, roughly chopped

a small handful of mint leaves, roughly chopped

50–100g roasted unsalted peanuts, chopped

for the dressing

2 tablespoons lime juice

I teaspoon caster sugar

I tablespoon fish sauce

I long red chilli (about the size of your index finger), deseeded and finely sliced

Ginger and Lime Cordial

We have had it drummed into us that we should be drinking at least two litres of water a day. Sometimes that can be a struggle, so to make it less of a chore, why not have a bottle of home-made cordial on hand to occasionally add to your water? It is packed full of vitamin C from the limes, while the ginger has numerous medicinal properties, from calming an upset tummy, alleviating the symptoms of colds or PMT to increasing your circulation. Can't go wrong really.

* **makes about 500m**

  **takes 45 minutes to make,
  including cooking time**

Place the ginger in a saucepan and bash it lightly with the end of a rolling pin to release the gingery juices.

Slice just one of the limes and add to the pan with 500ml water.

Bring the water to the boil, cover the pan with a lid and leave to simmer gently for 45 minutes. Remove the pan from the heat and stir in the sugar until it has dissolved.

Leave the cordial to cool, and then add the juice of the remaining limes. Strain the cordial through a sieve into a clean bottle.

This is now ready to use as you would a bought cordial — adding it to still, sparkling or soda water. If you have ice and a few wedges of lime to hand, it's even better.

125g fresh ginger, thinly sliced

3 plump, juicy unwaxed limes

300g granulated sugar

**still, sparkling or soda water,
 to serve**

PS ... *The cordial will last for weeks providing it is stored in a cool, dark place or in the fridge. An old cordial bottle or a funky glass bottle with a cork or flip-top lid is ideal to use, but do make sure you wash it out with very hot soapy water, rinse it well and dry before you fill it with the cordial.*

Does My Bum Look Big in This?
Food to tuck into without feeling guilty

Oh dear, been overdoing it again? Struggling with the top button on your fave pair of jeans, got a summer holiday to prepare yourself for or just having a 'fat' day? We've all been there (and will continue to go there). Once again, you hear yourself saying, 'Right, I'm going to eat really healthily from now on.'

Now, rather than hitting the supermarket for ready-made 'diet' foods or getting home armed with stacks of veggies and not knowing what to do with them, it's a good idea to have a few inspirational healthy recipes to turn to.

When I'm in one of these healthy moods, I like to cook well-balanced, nutritious and great-tasting dishes, full of fresh ingredients that won't make me feel bloated and overfull. It's not about losing weight, it's about finding recipes that make you feel good afterwards, which are uplifting, vitalizing and don't make your bum big. They also need to be quick to prepare so you aren't raiding the fridge for nibbles while you wait for the food to cook.

If you can't wait, then snack on some mixed seeds such as sunflower, pumpkin, linseed and sesame. They're great coated very lightly in soy sauce and sprinkled with chilli powder. Roast in a hot oven for about 5 minutes. Once cool, they will keep in an airtight container for days.

Gazpacho Salad

Chilled Spanish gazpacho soup is one of my favourite summery dishes because it contains so many fresh and tasty flavours. With this in mind, I have decided to transform those flavours into a simple salad, which is perfect for lunch or dinner.

* serves two
takes 20 to 25 minutes to make

Preheat the oven to 180°C/fan 160°C/gas 4.

Break the ciabatta into roughly 1cm pieces and scatter them on to a baking tray. Toss in a drizzle of olive oil and bake for about 5 minutes until they are just beginning to turn golden.

To make the dressing, place everything in a screw-top jar and shake well.

Peel the cucumber and slice it in half lengthways. Scoop out the seeds with a teaspoon, and then cut the cucumber into chunks. Mix the cucumber with the tomato, pepper, celery, onion, olives, basil and parsley.

If you're planning on eating this straight away, then add the ciabatta and toss everything together with the dressing. If you are packing this up to eat later, then keep the ciabatta and dressing separate from the rest of the salad and just mix everything together when you are ready to eat (the salad becomes soggy if it is left for too long).

PS . . . If this has whetted your appetite for a gazpacho soup, then simply blitz all of the ingredients, apart from the olives, in a blender with a handful of ice cubes. The olives, plus some finely chopped pepper, cucumber and tomato, can be scattered over the top to serve. Two recipes in one . . . bargain.

For the roasted pepper, you can place the pepper under the grill for 10 to 15 minutes, turning occasionally until it is charred all over. Put in a plastic sandwich bag and seal or place in a bowl and cover with clingfilm. Leave for about 10 minutes until it is cool enough to handle, and then peel away the skin and seeds. Alternatively you can buy a jar of ready roasted peppers.

for the salad

½ **ciabatta loaf**

olive oil

¼ **cucumber**

4–6 **really ripe tomatoes,**
   quartered and deseeded

1 **roasted red pepper, deseeded**
   and roughly chopped
   (see PS...)

1 **stick of celery, thinly sliced**

½ **small red onion,**
   thinly sliced

10–12 **black olives, stoned**

a handful of basil leaves

a handful of flat-leaf parsley
   leaves

for the dressing

2 **teaspoons sherry vinegar**

3 **tablespoons extra-virgin**
   olive oil

1 **clove of garlic**

sea salt and freshly ground
   black pepper

about 10 drops of Tabasco sauce

Green Minestrone

Looking down the list of ingredients and seeing all those green veggies, you just know this will be good for you. OK, so there is streaky bacon, but it adds great flavour and if you're really trying to cut down on fat, then you can use lean back bacon. Don't panic about the Parmesan; it has a strong flavour so you only need to grate a little over the top. Serve the soup straight away to make sure you get all of the goodness from the vegetables.

* serves four
   takes 30 to 35 minutes to make

Heat the olive oil in a large saucepan. Add the bacon and fry until it becomes golden. Stir in the spring onion, celery and leek until they start to soften. Add the garlic, cabbage, green beans and courgette and cook for 5 minutes, stirring occasionally.

Pour in the stock, bring to the boil and simmer for 5 minutes. Add the pasta and cook for the time stated on the packet. Season with salt and pepper and stir in the basil.

Ladle into large bowls, scatter with the Parmesan cheese and drizzle around a few drops of olive oil.

1 tablespoon olive oil

4–6 slices of smoked streaky bacon, cut into thin strips

1 bunch of spring onions, finely sliced

2 sticks of celery, finely sliced

1 leek, finely sliced

1 clove of garlic, crushed

½ small savoy cabbage, core removed and finely shredded

100g green beans, cut into 2cm sticks

1 courgette, finely chopped

750ml vegetable or chicken stock

75g tiny pasta shapes

sea salt and freshly ground black pepper

1 small bunch of basil leaves, shredded

grated Parmesan cheese

extra-virgin olive oil

Soy-glazed Sea Bass with Tomato and Ginger Relish

Sea bass is the perfect choice of fish for this recipe because it is wonderfully light and delicate. The superhealthy relish contains stacks of vitamins A and C and no added fats. If you want to go easy on the carbs, then serve with plenty of steamed broccoli, sugar snap peas or pak choi. If you want a more balanced meal, then Thai fragrant (jasmine) rice is a perfect partner.

* serves four

takes up to 40 minutes to make, including marinating time

Mix together the soy sauce and sugar. Add the sea bass, turning until it is coated with the mixture. Leave to marinate for about 20 to 30 minutes.

To make the relish, remove the green 'eye' from the tomatoes and roughly chop. Place in a saucepan with the ginger, garlic, sugar and vinegar. Bring to a simmer and cook for 20 to 25 minutes until you have a thick, relish consistency. Season with salt and pepper. The relish can be served either warm or cold.

Heat a frying pan with a trickle of the sesame or olive oil. Remove the sea bass from the marinade and fry for about 2 minutes on each side so that the fish is cooked through with a dark, sticky glaze. Serve with the tomato and ginger relish, steamed vegetables and/or some Thai fragrant (jasmine) rice.

for the sea bass
3 tablespoons soy sauce
2 tablespoons caster sugar
4 sea bass fillets, skinned
sesame or olive oil

for the relish
8 ripe tomatoes
1 knob (about 20g) of fresh ginger, peeled and finely chopped or grated
1 clove of garlic, crushed or chopped
1½ tablespoons caster sugar
1 teaspoon rice vinegar or white wine vinegar
sea salt and freshly ground black pepper

PS . . . *The relish can be made in advance and kept in the fridge for up to a week. Any leftover relish is delicious with cheese, cold meats or in burgers.*

Pan-fried Mackerel with Beetroot, Avocado and Potato Salad

Mackerel is a superhealthy ingredient to cook because it contains more omega-3 fatty acids than any other fish (excellent for brainpower and lowering your cholesterol levels). You might even look younger after eating this dish — the avocado is a brilliant anti-ageing food because of the amount of vitamin E it contains.

* serves four
takes about 25 minutes to make

Cook the potatoes in boiling salted water until they are tender. Drain, leave to cool, and then cut into chunks, either leaving the skin on for extra goodness or peeling them first.

While the potatoes are boiling, toast the sunflower seeds in a frying pan for a couple of minutes until they are just becoming golden and crunchy. Remove from the pan and leave to cool.

Place the cooled potatoes in a bowl and mix with the toasted sunflower seeds, avocado, beetroot, capers, lemon zest and juice, chives or spring onions and crème fraîche. Season with salt and pepper and lightly mix together.

Heat a trickle of olive oil in a frying pan over a high heat. Season the mackerel with salt and pepper and fry in the pan for just a few minutes each side until golden. Squeeze over the lemon juice and serve with the salad.

for the salad

250g new potatoes

3 tablespoons sunflower seeds

1 large ripe avocado, chopped

200g cooked beetroot, chopped

2 tablespoons capers

finely grated zest of 1 lemon

a good squeeze of lemon juice

1 tablespoon chopped chives or 3 finely chopped spring onions

2 tablespoons low-fat crème fraîche

sea salt and freshly ground black pepper

for the mackerel

olive oil

4–8 mackerel fillets (depending on their size)

sea salt and freshly ground black pepper

a squeeze of lemon juice

Duck, Orange and Honey Stir-fry with Lots of Greens

Duck meat is surprisingly high in all of the B vitamins, but if duck doesn't rock your wok, just substitute it with chicken, beef or pork. Quickly cooking the green veggies in a wok is one of the best ways of maintaining as many of their health benefits as possible. If you are feeling really hungry, throw in some cooked noodles towards the end of the cooking time or serve with brown rice.

* **serves two**

takes 25 minutes to make, plus 30 minutes marinating time

Mix together the orange zest, garlic, ginger, soy sauce and honey in a bowl. Add the duck strips and leave to marinate for up to 30 minutes.

Heat a wok over a high heat. Add the sesame seeds and toss around until they are lightly golden. Remove from the pan and return the pan to the heat. Add 1 tablespoon of the oil and when it is beginning to smoke, remove the duck from the marinade (leaving behind as much marinade in the dish as possible) and add to the wok. Stir-fry for a few minutes until it's browned and sticky, and then transfer to a plate.

Add all of the vegetables to the wok with a little extra oil if it looks like it needs it. Stir-fry for about 3 minutes. Mix the orange juice into the remaining marinade and pour in. Cook for a couple of minutes longer for the sauce to thicken and the vegetables to become almost tender. Return the duck to the wok, stir, and then spoon into bowls and scatter with the sesame seeds.

grated zest and juice of ½ small orange

2 cloves of garlic, crushed

1 knob (about 15g) of fresh ginger, peeled and finely chopped or grated

1 tablespoon dark soy sauce

2 tablespoons honey

1 large or 2 small skinless duck breasts, cut into strips

1 tablespoon sesame seeds

1–2 tablespoons sunflower or vegetable oil

2 pak choi, cut into quarters lengthways

100g thin asparagus tips

200g Chinese, tenderstem or traditional broccoli

1 bunch of spring onions, cut into 2–3cm pieces

PS . . . *If you eat this stir-fry with chopsticks, then you'll eat slower, which is better for your digestion. What's more, you'll feel fuller afterwards.*

Superfruit Salad

There are a number of superfoods that we should all be trying to eat on a regular basis for their health-giving, disease-preventing properties. A brilliant way to enjoy some is to tuck into this vibrant 'superfruit' salad, crammed full of vitamins, minerals and antioxidants. The addition of a sweet mango and orange purée to the chopped fruit makes this extra fruity.

* serves four
   takes 15 to 20 minutes to make

Place the mango, orange juice and a splash of orange liqueur, if you are using it, in a blender and blitz until you have a smooth purée.

Place the strawberries, kiwi, blueberries, pineapple and shredded mint in a large bowl and gently stir in the purée. Spoon into bowls and serve.

1 small ripe mango, peeled and stone removed

juice of 1 orange

a splash of Cointreau or Grand Marnier (for a treat)

100g strawberries

2–3 kiwi fruit, peeled, halved and sliced

100g blueberries

1 small pineapple, peeled and chopped (core removed if it seems tough)

a few mint leaves, shredded

PS . . . *If you don't use all of the mango purée for the fruit salad, it is delicious stirred into natural or Greek yoghurt.*

Diet...What Diet?
Posh nosh to impress

OK, so you're in the mood for being healthy, but also love entertaining and having friends round for dinner. Dinner parties and healthy food aren't an obvious partnership — in fact they can seem like chalk and cheese to many people. It's at these times that you can find your mind going totally blank trying to think of what to serve without pushing the fact that you want to eat healthy food. After all, do you really want to shout about the fact that you've been struggling with the top button on your jeans all day?

Well, don't despair. It's amazing what delicious dishes can be created that won't make you feel at all guilty and aren't obviously healthy. Certain cooking methods, such as steaming, poaching and grilling, are brilliant for cutting out added fats and by using fresh, full-of-flavour ingredients, you can serve up extremely tasty food.

To follow are some well-balanced main courses, plus a gorgeous soup and a yummy dessert that are delicious, stylish and impressive for your guests. By being creative with the food and presentation, your guests will never know that you're watching what you eat.

What about before dinner I hear you say, when the crisps and naughty nibbles come out with a predinner drink? Well, it's still possible to have nibbles without them being full of salt and fat. I like to take a selection of nuts such as almonds, brazils and walnuts (all full of great essential nutrients) and coat them in a lightly whisked egg white, pinch of salt and a mixture of spices (chilli powder and cumin, Chinese five-spice or garam masala are all great flavours). Roast them on a baking tray for about 10 minutes and, once cool, break up and serve.

If you can't survive without a dip before dinner, then whiz up some avocado, rocket, red chilli and lemon juice. Serve with tortillas cut into wedges and grilled until crispy — a much healthier version of bought tortilla crisps.

Miso Salmon with Asian Rice Salad

If you're in the mood for something summery and rather impressive, then you must give this a go. The miso paste has a rich, naturally salty flavour, which adds a wonderful depth and character to foods, especially fish. Give your brain a boost with the omega-3 rich salmon or try a piece of cod, sea bass, sea bream, mackerel or trout.

❋ serves four
takes about 45 minutes to make

First of all, marinate the salmon. Mix together the miso paste, honey and mirin. Spread over the salmon fillets and leave them to marinate while you make the salad, turning the fish halfway through.

To make the salad, place the rice in a sieve and rinse under cold water for a couple of minutes (this removes any excess starch, which can make the cooked rice gloopy and heavy). Place the rice in a saucepan with a pinch of salt and 550ml water. Bring to the boil and cover with a tight-fitting lid. Reduce the heat to low and leave the rice to cook for 10 minutes before removing the pan from the heat. Don't lift off the lid. Just leave the rice to continue cooking in the pan for a further 5 to 10 minutes. Fluff up the rice with a fork, and then tip out on to a baking tray, loosely spreading it to cool down. The rice should only take about 15 minutes to reach room temperature.

Once the rice is cold, gently heat the rice vinegar, caster sugar and a pinch of salt in a small pan, stirring until the sugar has dissolved. Transfer the rice to a large bowl and stir in the sweetened rice vinegar, spring onion, cucumber, chilli and herbs. The salad is now ready.

Preheat the grill to high. Transfer the salmon to a baking tray and spoon over any marinade. Grill for 5 to 6 minutes until the salmon is golden and only just cooked through, maintaining a succulent centre. Serve straight away with the salad.

for the salmon

4 teaspoons miso paste

2 teaspoons runny honey

2 teaspoons mirin

4 salmon fillets

for the salad

400g Thai fragrant (jasmine) rice

sea salt

4 tablespoons rice vinegar

2 tablespoons caster sugar

1 bunch of spring onions, finely sliced

½ cucumber, halved lengthways, deseeded and finely sliced

2 long red chillies, halved, deseeded and finely sliced

a large handful each of basil, mint and coriander leaves

In the mood for a drink? *Go for a fruity Verdelho or a Riesling to match the texture of the fish and handle the herbs and spices.*

Chilled Watermelon, Red Pepper and Chilli Soup

This refreshing soup makes a great starter or a light lunch for the summer. Don't be put off by having to grill your own peppers, they take hardly any time at all, but if you are stretched, then buy a jar of some already done. They aren't quite as flavourful, but they are a great speedy alternative.

* serves four

takes about 30 minutes to make, plus 2 hours to chill

Preheat the grill to high.

Grill the peppers for 10 to 15 minutes, turning occasionally until they are charred all over. Put them in a plastic sandwich bag and seal or place in a bowl and cover with clingfilm. Leave the peppers for about 10 minutes until they are cool enough to handle, and then peel away the skins and seeds.

Place the grilled peppers into a food processor or blender with the watermelon, chilli, garlic, red wine vinegar, large basil leaves and some salt and pepper and blitz until you have a very smooth soup. Pass through a sieve to remove the watermelon pips and place in the fridge for at least 2 hours until it is totally chilled. To save time, you can place it in the freezer for 30 minutes, stirring occasionally.

To serve the soup, spoon it into bowls, add a twist of pepper and scatter over the small basil leaves and feta cheese. Finally, drizzle a little olive oil around the edge of each bowl.

2 red peppers

1kg watermelon, cut into chunks (giving you about 600g flesh)

1 long red chilli, deseeded and roughly chopped

1 small clove of garlic, crushed

1½ tablespoons red wine vinegar

8 large basil leaves

sea salt and freshly ground black pepper

small basil leaves to garnish

cubes of feta cheese to garnish

olive oil

PS . . . *The soup is great as it is, but you can also replace the feta cheese with some of these tasty additions:* * *Sliced black olives.* * *Grilled prosciutto, Parma ham or serrano ham.* * *A spoonful of low-fat crème fraîche.*

In the mood for a drink? *A chilled rosé packed with fruit and zip hits the spot every time.*

Steamed Lemon and Tarragon Chicken with Baby Vegetable Broth

This tastes so great it's hard to believe it's so good for you. Steaming the chicken is a really healthy method of cooking. It doesn't require any oil or fat and the chicken will be deliciously juicy and tender. Any juices or marinade from the chicken go straight into the broth, which is cooking in the saucepan below with the baby vegetables.

* serves four

**takes about 25 minutes to make,
plus up to 1 hour marinating time**

Slash the chicken breasts several times with a sharp knife and place in a flat dish. Mix together the zest and juice of the lemon with the tarragon sprigs, garlic and seasoning. Pour over the chicken and leave to marinate for 30 minutes to 1 hour if you have time. If not, just 10 minutes will be fine.

Pour the stock and wine into the bottom part of a steamer or a saucepan, add the tomato purée and bring to the boil.

Remove the chicken from the marinade and place in the steamer top. Sit over the bottom part of the steamer or the saucepan and cover with a lid. Steam for just 5 minutes, and then drop the courgette, carrot, baby corn and shallots into the boiling broth. Once the broth has returned to the boil, replace the steamer top and continue steaming the chicken for a further 5 minutes.

The chicken should now be cooked through and wonderfully juicy. Take off the heat and put to one side to rest. Add the peas, mangetout or sugar snaps and the asparagus to the broth and boil for 2 minutes with the lid off.

Divide the vegetables into four bowls. Season the broth with salt if needed and ladle over the vegetables. Sit the chicken on top, scatter over the tarragon leaves and serve immediately while steaming hot.

for the chicken

4 skinless chicken breasts

**finely grated zest and juice
of 1 small lemon**

4 sprigs of tarragon

1 clove of garlic, crushed

**sea salt and freshly ground
black pepper**

for the broth

900ml chicken stock

150ml white wine

1 teaspoon tomato purée

**150g baby courgettes,
halved lengthways**

**150g baby carrots (with tops
on if possible), halved
lengthways if they're thick**

**100g baby corn,
halved lengthways**

**4–6 shallots, peeled and sliced
into slim wedges**

175g frozen peas, defrosted

100g mangetout

100g thin asparagus tips

sea salt

a small handful of tarragon

Beef Tagine with Radish and Parsley Salad

This classic combination of sweet and spicy flavours in a rich sauce is unbelievably delicious and even though it takes a while to cook, it is very simple to prepare and has no added fat whatsoever.

* serves four

takes about 20 minutes to make, plus 2 hours to cook

Put the beef into a tagine if you want to be really authentic (although a casserole or heavy-based saucepan will do the job just as well). Stir in the onion, garlic, ginger, cumin, cinnamon, saffron and harissa paste and season with salt and pepper. Pour over the stock or water and bring to a simmer. Cover with a lid and gently simmer for 1½ hours or until the meat is really tender.

Add the prunes and tomato to the tagine and simmer uncovered for a further 30 minutes or until the sauce has thickened.

To make the salad, mix everything together and place in a shallow bowl or plate. If the radishes have nice green tops on them, keep these attached as they have a great flavour.

Taste the tagine for seasoning, adding salt and pepper if it is needed, and stir in the parsley. Scatter over the pistachios and serve with the salad.

PS . . . *For a change, you can easily replace the beef with cubes of boneless shoulder of lamb, and then use lamb rather than beef stock. Swap the prunes for apricots.*

If you can't get hold of any harissa paste, then a good pinch of chilli powder can be used instead.

In the mood for a drink? *The big spicy flavours in this dish will soak up a luscious Shiraz or an Argentinian Malbec.*

for the tagine

1kg braising steak, trimmed of fat and cubed

1 onion, chopped

2 cloves of garlic, crushed

1 large knob (about 25g) of fresh ginger, peeled and grated

1 teaspoon ground cumin

½ teaspoon ground cinnamon

a small pinch of saffron

1 teaspoon harissa paste

sea salt and freshly ground black pepper

650ml beef stock or water

175g prunes, halved

2 large ripe tomatoes, peeled and chopped

2 tablespoons chopped parsley

75g shelled and halved pistachios

for the salad

300g radishes

4–6 ripe, juicy tomatoes, cut into wedges

1 small red onion

1 good-sized bunch of flat-leaf parsley, roughly chopped

juice of ½ lemon

2 tablespoons olive oil

sea salt and freshly ground black pepper

Lamb Steaks with Pea and Chickpea Mash and Mint and Lemon Pesto

Any cut of lamb can be used for this but I like leg steaks because they are lean, quick to cook and reasonably priced. Chickpeas are a great source of low-fat protein, the pesto is deceivingly healthy because it contains vitamin E-rich almonds and extra-virgin olive oil, while the mint is great for your digestion.

* **serves four**
  takes about 20 minutes to make

Preheat the oven to 180°C/fan 160°C/gas 4.

Firstly, to make the pesto spread the almonds on a baking sheet and toast in the oven until they are golden. This will only take a few minutes, so keep your eye on them as they can burn quickly.

Once the almonds are toasted, cool, and then tip into a blender or small food processor. Add the mint, parsley, lemon zest, oil and Parmesan. Blitz until you have a rough paste and season.

To make the mash, bring the stock to the boil in a saucepan. Add the peas and boil for 2 minutes. Stir in the chickpeas and cook until they are heated through. Remove from the heat, add the paprika and lemon juice and season with salt and pepper. Roughly mash with a potato masher or briefly whiz in a food processor. Keep warm while you cook the steaks.

Season the lamb steaks with salt and pepper. Heat a trickle of olive oil in a frying pan to a medium-high heat. Add the lamb and cook for 6 minutes, turning halfway through. This will cook them to medium, so cook for 1 to 2 minutes longer if you prefer well done meat or, of course, less if you like it rarer. Once the lamb is cooked to your liking, leave it to rest for a few minutes. The lamb can now be served with the mash and a good spoonful of the pesto.

for the pesto

50g almonds, flaked or chopped

20g mint leaves

10g parsley

grated zest of 1 lemon

125ml extra-virgin olive oil

15g grated Parmesan cheese

sea salt and freshly ground black pepper

for the lamb and mash

250ml chicken stock

250g frozen peas

2 x 400g tins of chickpeas, drained

1 teaspoon paprika

a good squeeze of lemon juice

sea salt and freshly ground black pepper

4 lamb leg steaks

olive oil

PS . . . *To complete the dish, I often roast or grill some cherry tomatoes on the vine for a few minutes.*

48 * healthy

Rosé Poached Pear

Your guests won't be impressed with a portion of healthy fruit or yoghurt, but most dinner party puddings seem a little bit too naughty when you are trying to be good. This, however, looks great and has such a full flavour you'll convince even yourself that it must be unhealthy. OK, so it has wine in it, but the alcohol will be boiled away and there really is very little added sugar when you consider this serves four people. Put it this way — it's better for you than a cheesecake.

* serves four
takes about 30 to 35 minutes to make

Place the rosé, sugar, honey and vanilla pod into a saucepan and bring to a gentle simmer. Add the pears and, unless they are totally submerged in the poaching liquid, cut out some greaseproof paper to fit inside the pan and sit on top of them. Simmer for 8 minutes or until the pears feel tender when tested with a skewer. They may need a little longer if they aren't very ripe.

Lift the pears out with a slotted spoon to drain and bring the poaching liquid to the boil. Boil for 15–20 minutes (depending on how wide your pan is) until you have a loose, syrupy consistency. Leave to cool (this will be quicker if you pour the liquid into a cool jug, bowl or pan).

Remove the vanilla pod from the syrup and serve the pears with the syrup spooned over them and a sprig of mint, nice fruity sorbet or dollop of crème fraîche if you fancy.

500ml rosé wine

75g sugar

2 tablespoons runny honey

1 vanilla pod, split

4 ripe, juicy pears, peeled, halved and cores removed

sprig of mint, fruity sorbet or low fat crème fraîche, to serve (optional)

PS . . . *If you can, leave the stalk attached to one half of each pear because it looks really lovely when you serve them.*

In the mood for a drink? *A chilled rosé is a must.*

In the Mood for Something
Naughty but Nice

BEWARE — this chapter could seriously expand your waistline.

Ooh — naughty moods, they're the evil ones, when the little 'mind' devils pester you until they're satisfied, demanding something chocolaty, sugary, creamy, basically anything that's bad for you.

Both sweet and savoury 'naughty but nice' foods can be craved for when you're in that kind of mood, but I decided to fill this chapter with perhaps the naughtier of the two: sweet things.

There are numerous reasons for desiring 'naughty but nice' food. PMT is definitely up at the top with us girls (chocolate usually being the most craved thing) and no, it's not just an excuse to eat more chocolate — there's evidence! Apparently our bodies can lack magnesium during times of PMT, which is something chocolate is rich in, therefore we want to eat it. And there's more. When PMT strikes, the hormone progesterone is higher than usual, which triggers cravings for fatty foods. So that's the ladies sorted. What's your excuse, or should I say 'reason', boys?

Often, if we're bored, our minds drift to naughty food. More often than not, it's in the afternoon that a tasty sweet treat is required (well, you have been working hard). Usually this is because our

blood-sugar levels dip in the afternoon and our brain tells us we need sugar fast, putting us in a grumpy or irritable mood. Eating something sweet will uplift your mood, making you feel good. Now, rather than hitting the vending machine or nearest newsagent in desperation to buy overprocessed, excessively sugary snacks, treat yourself to some home-made goodies that aren't so sweet that your cravings come back within minutes of satisfying them.

There are also times when I want total decadence in the form of naughty but nice foods. This is often when I have a night in on my own watching the latest chick flick or reality TV show or have a bunch of girls round for a catch-up (that way you can share the guilt). Ice cream and naughty puddings are called for here.

But really, why should we need a reason to justify our mood for wanting to eat naughty but nice food? If your mood calls for it, and so long as you don't eat it all day every day, go for it.

Chocoholic Dreams
Putting a smile on every chocolate-lover's face

I love chocolate. I wouldn't say I'm a chocoholic, but I do enjoy tucking into a nice chocolaty pudding, cake, biscuit or drink when the mood arises. I do, however, know some people who will do ANYTHING for chocolate, so these recipes are for them and anyone else out there who can't survive without their chocolate fix.

A craving for chocolate can strike at any time of the night or day apparently because it contains substances similar to drugs, which can make it addictive and act as a stimulant, antidepressant or mood-enhancer. So, that might explain why you're in the mood for chocolate when you're feeling down or blue. There are times though when I'm in the mood for something chocolaty for no reason at all and these cheeky cravings do have a habit of catching me out. One of my favourite quick solutions is to make an iced chocolate milkshake. It's so delicious and really quick to put together. All I do is melt some milk chocolate with a splash of milk in the microwave, and then blitz it in a liquidizer with a few ice cubes and enough milk to fill a glass. You can make it as chocolaty as you like, but I find five or six squares of chocolate is usually enough for a glass of milk. If I am feeling really naughty, I add a dollop of whipped cream on top.

In fact, while I am on the subject of whipping something up, home-made chocolate and almond croissants are great for morning chocolate cravings. OK, so when I say home-made that's not strictly true because all you do is split a bought croissant in half, fill it with some chopped chocolate and toasted flaked almonds and bake in the oven until the chocolate is all gooey in the centre. These are fantastic and hit the spot every time.

Saucy Chocolate Raspberry Puddings

These are a perfect emergency pud for chocoholics because they are so unbelievably easy to throw together. The best bit is that they create their own silky smooth chocolate sauce below the rich gooey sponge. I bet you can't wait.

* **makes four**
  takes 20 minutes to cook

Preheat the oven to 180°C/fan 160°C/gas 4.

Grease four 300ml (or thereabouts) ovenproof dishes, cups, ramekins or pudding basins.

Sift the flour, salt, baking powder and cocoa powder into a bowl and beat in the caster sugar, milk, melted butter, eggs and Grand Marnier or Cointreau until you have a smooth batter. Stir in the raspberries and divide among the pudding moulds.

In a separate bowl, mix together the soft brown sugar and cocoa powder. Sprinkle this over the top of the puddings, and then pour a quarter of the boiling water over the top of each one, making sure there is about a 1cm gap at the top of the dishes to allow for rising.

Sit on a baking tray and cook for 20 minutes. Remove from the oven and leave to sit for about 5 minutes, then serve with thick cream, crème fraîche or vanilla ice cream.

for the puddings
125g plain flour
a pinch of salt
1 tablespoon baking powder
4 tablespoons cocoa powder
125g caster sugar
250ml milk
75g unsalted butter, melted
2 large eggs, lightly beaten
1 tablespoon Grand Marnier or Cointreau (optional)
100g raspberries (fresh or defrosted frozen ones)

for the sauce
125g soft brown sugar
1½ tablespoons cocoa powder
150ml boiling water

PS . . . *For a different flavour, replace the raspberries with 75g chopped nuts (walnuts, brazils, pecans or hazelnuts) and use brandy or whisky instead of the Grand Marnier or Cointreau.*

In the mood for a drink? *How about trying a sparkling Shiraz (red and sparkly — great for a change).*

Triple Chocolate Hit

In other words, a rich chocolate tart with chocolate orange pastry and malted milk chocolate ice cream, and if that sounds full on, believe me, it is. It's the Ferrari of chocolate puddings and the best dessert for absolute chocoholics everywhere. The recipe is made in three straightforward stages, so please don't be put off by the length. The ice cream can be made days in advance and the tart hours before you want to serve it.

* **serves six to eight**

  takes about 1 hour to make the tart and between 20 minutes and 4½ hours to freeze the ice cream (depending on whether you have an ice cream machine or not)

Stage 1 – the ice cream

Bring the milk to the boil in a non-stick saucepan and then stir in the Horlicks.

Beat the egg yolks with the caster sugar until they are thickened, pale and creamy. Pour over the malted milk and stir well. Return to the pan and cook over a gentle heat, stirring all of the time, until the mixture is thick enough to coat the back of the spoon (about the consistency of double cream). Make sure you don't boil the custard because it may separate and curdle. If you feel it is getting too hot, remove from the heat and just continue stirring until it thickens. Stir in the chocolate until it has melted, cover the surface directly with clingfilm and leave to cool. Once cool, stir in the cream and freeze following the instructions on page 91.

Stage 2 – the pastry

Sift the flour and cocoa powder into a food processor and blitz with the butter to form fine crumbs. Add the sugar and orange zest, and then gradually add the milk, processing briefly to form a soft dough. Wrap the dough in clingfilm and chill for 30 minutes or longer.

Heat the oven to 180°C/fan 160°C/gas 4.

for the ice cream

250ml milk

2 tablespoons Horlicks powder

2 large egg yolks

50g caster sugar

150g milk chocolate, broken into pieces

150ml double cream

for the pastry

125g plain flour

20g cocoa powder

65g unsalted butter, chilled and cut into cubes

2½ tablespoons caster sugar

grated zest of 1 orange

about 2 tablespoons milk

(continued on page 58)

Thinly roll out the chilled pastry on a well-floured surface and line an approximately 22cm loose-bottomed shallow tart tin. Don't worry if you have any gaps or cracks in the pastry because they can be filled with the pastry trimmings. Cover with a piece of greaseproof paper and fill with a layer of baking beans or rice. Cook for 15 minutes. Remove the paper and cook for a further 5 minutes until the pastry is just becoming golden.

Stage 3 – the filling

Whisk the eggs yolks and egg with the sugar until very pale, thick and creamy. Using an electric whisk will be much quicker (and less tiring) than doing it by hand.

Melt the butter and dark chocolate either in a bowl over a pan of simmering water or gently in the microwave. Add to the egg mixture and fold together until completely combined. Pour into the pastry case and bake for 10 minutes (the filling will still be slightly wobbly, but will set when it cools). Remove from the oven and cool completely. To maintain the gooey filling texture, the tart needs to be kept at room temperature.

To serve this chocolate feast, sprinkle over grated chocolate or dust the tart with cocoa powder (yes – more chocolate), cut into wedges and sit each one on a plate with a spoon of the malted milk ice cream next to it.

for the filling

3 large egg yolks

1 large egg

50g caster sugar

150g unsalted butter

200g dark chocolate (70% cocoa solids), chopped

1 tablespoon grated chocolate or cocoa powder

PS... *If there is any tart left over, it can be stored in the fridge for a couple of days. The filling will firm up, making it perfect to wrap up and take a slice into work the next day.*

What are you going to do with those egg whites? Why not turn to page 71 and make the little coconut and raspberry cakes.

In the mood for a drink? *If you dare, try the choc 'n' nut liqueur on page 62 for a bigger chocolate feast.*

White Chocolate and Bailey's Cheesecake

Now this is what I call rich, so much so that you will probably only manage one slice, which is saying something for chocolate fans. It's perfect to serve as a dessert, mid-morning with coffee, for afternoon tea or...well, to be honest, you could eat this any time.

* **makes about ten to twelve slices**
  takes 45 minutes to bake

Preheat the oven to 180°C/fan 160°C/gas 4.

First grease a round 22 to 24cm springform or loose-bottomed cake tin and line the base with greaseproof paper.

To make the base, finely crush the biscuits until they resemble fine breadcrumbs. This is best done in a food processor, but can be done by putting them in a sealed freezer bag and bashing with a rolling pin (a great way to relieve any stress!) Mix in the ground almonds, ginger and melted butter. Press well into the base of the cake tin and refrigerate.

Beat the cream cheese, sugar and cornflour (ideally in a food processor or using an electric hand whisk). Add in the eggs, cream and Bailey's and beat until you have a smooth, creamy consistency. Stir in the white chocolate.

Pour into the tin and sit in a roasting tray filled with 1 to 2cm of hot water. Cook in the oven for 45 minutes until the top is lightly golden and the filling is just set. Remove from the oven and leave to cool before taking out of the tin.

Serve cut into slices as big or small as you can manage.

for the base

250g shortbread biscuits

100g ground almonds

2 teaspoons ground ginger

75g melted butter

for the filling

675g cream cheese (low-fat or full-fat – it's up to you)

200g caster sugar

3 tablespoons cornflour

2 large eggs, beaten

150ml whipping cream

150ml Bailey's

125g white chocolate, chopped

In the mood for a drink? *A sweet dessert wine or a sparkling number such as an Asti Spumante, which is wonderful with rich, sweet desserts (don't be a snob, there's more to life than Champagne).*

Choc 'n' Nut Liqueur

I have to admit it, I occasionally turn to a glass of Bailey's after a meal when I don't want the punch from a whisky or brandy or a glass of sweet, sticky liqueur. Recently, I was after something new to try and came up with this simple and impressive alternative. It's rich, indulgent and the taste lingers for ages afterwards. It's also really great poured over ice cream for ultimate naughtiness.

* **makes about 800ml**
  takes 10 minutes to make

Melt the chocolate and cream either in a bowl over a pan of simmering water or gently in the microwave. Stir well until the mixture is smooth, cover with clingfilm, and then leave to cool.

Once it's cool, stir in the liqueur and pour into a clean bottle. Store at room temperature and shake the bottle lightly before using.

Serve neat, poured over ice or, for something a little different, pour over ice cream as a dessert. The liqueur should last for a few weeks if you don't drink it all before then.

200g milk chocolate, broken into pieces

300ml single cream

400ml amaretto or Frangelico liqueur

ice or ice cream, to serve

PS . . . *You can try this with almost any liqueur: coffee, orange, coconut, even brandy or whisky.*

Creamy Hot Chocolate Orange

Are you in the mood for a warming mug of hot chocolate? This is a real treat — one I got a taste for when I first went skiing. It certainly helped me down the slopes on chilly afternoons.

* **makes enough for four mugs**
  takes 10 minutes to make

Place the milk, cream and orange zest in a saucepan and gently bring to the boil. Remove from the heat and stir in the chocolate until it has completely dissolved. Add the Cointreau or Grand Marnier and some sugar if you like it a little sweeter. Remove the orange zest.

Pour into mugs, add a dollop of whipped cream and grate over the chocolate to serve.

600ml milk

100ml single cream

zest of 1 orange

125g dark chocolate
   (70% cocoa solids), chopped

a splash of Cointreau or
   Grand Marnier
      (as generous as you like)

sugar, to taste

whipped cream and extra
   chocolate, to grate over the top

PS... *A good splash of brandy or rum also works very well.*

Chocolate, Cherry and Walnut Brownies

These are to die for! I have had so much enjoyment (as you can imagine) trying out different versions of brownies and I think these tick all the boxes — rich, not too sweet, a little bit fruity and a little bit nutty, gooey in the middle with a crisp top.

* **makes nine to twelve good-sized brownies**
  takes about 25 minutes to bake

Preheat the oven to 180°C/fan 160°C/gas 4.

Grease and line an approximately 20 by 30cm rectangular baking tin, 3 to 4cm deep, with greaseproof or parchment paper. Melt the butter and chocolate either in a bowl over a pan of simmering water or gently in the microwave.

With an electric hand whisk, beat together the eggs, sugar and vanilla extract until they are lovely and thick and creamy. Mix in the melted chocolate and butter. Finally stir in the flour, salt, cherries and walnuts.

Pour into the baking tin and cook for about 25 minutes until the top is cracking and the centre is just set. Leave to cool in the tin for about 20 minutes before cutting into squares.

Serve warm or, if you can resist leaving them, cold.

200g unsalted butter

200g dark chocolate (70% cocoa solids), chopped

3 large eggs

300g granulated sugar

2 teaspoons vanilla extract

125g plain flour

a pinch of salt

100g dried cherries

100g walnut pieces

PS . . . *If you're a hard-core chocoholic, you can have a double-chocolate fix by adding 150g chopped milk or white chocolate chunks to the mixture before baking.*

To serve the brownies as a dessert, whip up a delicious orange mascarpone cream to serve with them. Beat together 200g mascarpone, 50g sifted icing sugar and the finely grated zest of 1 small orange until you have a smooth, creamy mixture. If it seems too thick, just beat in some milk to loosen. Serve a big spoonful on top of the warm brownies so it melts over them.

White Chocolate and Macadamia Cookies

These melt-in-the-mouth cookies are definitely for those with a sweet tooth. If you want to go for double chocolate and macadamia cookies, then check out the PS at the bottom of the recipe.

* **makes about twelve**
  takes about 20 minutes to make

Preheat the oven to 180°C/fan 160°C/gas 4.

Beat together the butter and sugar until it is pale and creamy, either in an electric mixer or, if you are feeling energetic, by hand. Beat in the vanilla extract and egg yolk. Add the flour, white chocolate chunks and chopped nuts. Mix until you have a smooth dough, with the only lumps being the chocolate and nuts.

Using your hands, roll the dough into golf-sized balls and lightly press each one flat on to a greased baking sheet, making sure they are spread slightly apart.

Bake for 12 minutes until golden. Remove from the oven and let cool for a couple of minutes before either eating or cooling completely on a wire rack.

125g butter, softened

85g soft light brown sugar

1 teaspoon vanilla extract

1 large egg yolk

150g plain flour

75g white chocolate, chopped or broken into small chunks

50g macadamia nuts, chopped

PS . . . To make these extra chocolaty, replace 25g of the flour with 15g of cocoa powder.

Sweet Cravings
Treats for any time of the day

Oh yes, it's that time of the day when you are in a 'low' and want something sweet to satisfy your cravings. It's usually in the afternoon (when your desk looks like a bed), but it can quite easily hit you midmorning or even late at night. Your blood-sugar levels are low and you're begging for sugar.

I know there are plenty of superhealthy things we should eat during the day to prevent these cravings from ever happening, but in the real world we don't always do as we're told and we end up having to satisfy our mood for a sweet treat. Anyhow, it's much more fun being in a naughty mood and sinking your teeth into a cake, pastry or biscuit, especially when you have made it yourself. So much satisfaction and pleasure can be gained from cooking your own sweet treats, it somehow takes away a bit of the guilt.

Forget big puddings here. This is all about little treats to indulge yourself with as an alternative to reaching for a packet of bought biscuits or that greasy doughnut.

Apricot Danish

The best thing about these apricot Danish is that they use really accessible ingredients and are easy to make, so you can tuck into them whenever the mood arises. I prefer these to bought Danish pastries, which I usually find are far too sweet and definitely not as fresh and crisp-tasting.

* makes eight
takes about 20 to 25 minutes to make

Preheat the oven to 200°C/fan 180°C/gas 6.

Cut the pastry into eight squares. Brush the surfaces with some of the egg yolk and milk (the egg wash) and spoon the custard into the middle of each one.

Slice each apricot into three and lay the slices, one behind the other, in a diagonal line from one corner of each square to the opposite corner.

Scatter over the almonds and dust very generously with icing sugar.

Take the other two corners of each square and fold over so that the tips join, brushing them with a little egg wash and pinching to seal together.

Finally, brush any pastry showing with the egg wash and dust with a little more icing sugar. Bake for 12 to 15 minutes until golden.

Remove from the oven and either serve warm or gently reheat when needed.

375g ready-rolled puff pastry

1 egg yolk mixed with
   1 tablespoon milk

5-6 tablespoons bought
   ready-made custard

400g tin of apricot halves in
   syrup, drained

5 tablespoons flaked almonds

8 tablespoons icing sugar

PS...*You don't have to stick to apricots; tinned peaches or pears can be used or thinly sliced fresh fruits such as apples, plums or strawberries.*

In the mood for a drink? *A frothy cappuccino is the perfect match.*

Little Coconut and Raspberry Cakes

Delicious . . . that is the only word I can use to describe these. They look so cute you won't want to stop at just one, believe me.

* makes twelve
takes about 15 minutes to bake

Preheat the oven to 180°C/fan 160°C/gas 4.

Line a muffin tin with twelve paper muffin cases.

This couldn't be easier. Simply mix together everything, apart from the raspberries, until smooth. Spoon into the paper cases and divide the raspberries among the cakes, pressing them lightly on to the surface. Bake for 15 minutes, until the cakes are golden and just springy to touch in the middle.

Remove from the oven and cool slightly before removing from the tin. Serve warm or cold.

The cakes will keep in an airtight container for a few days and still remain really moist and yummy.

125g unsalted butter, melted
25g ground almonds
75g desiccated coconut
275g icing sugar, sifted
75g plain flour
½ teaspoon baking powder
5 large egg whites
100g raspberries

PS . . . *If you fancy, you can also use blueberries, small strawberries or blackberries instead of raspberries. Frozen raspberries are perfect to use when fresh ones are out of season.*

In the mood for a drink? *Fruit tea (a healthy drink that'll help you feel less guilty if you have more than one cake).*

Cocoa and Cinnamon-sugared Popcorn

If you want a quick bit of fun in the kitchen, then give this popcorn a go. It takes no time at all and has a wonderful flavour. Even better, it doesn't have too much sugar so it won't stick your teeth together like a lot of bought popcorn does. I like to think of this recipe as a 'mildly naughty and extremely nice' recipe.

* **serves two to four**
  takes about 10 minutes to make

Stir together the sugar, cinnamon and cocoa powder and keep to one side.

Heat a large saucepan over a high heat. Add enough oil to just cover the bottom of the pan. Stir in the popcorn until it is coated in the oil. Cover the pan with a lid and wait a minute or two for the popping to start. Shake the pan a couple of times while the corn pops, and as soon as the popping stops, remove from the pan from the heat.

Sprinkle over the chocolate cinnamon sugar. Stir thoroughly until the popcorn is coated and the sugar is dissolving and sticking to the popcorn. Leave for a few minutes for the sugar to cool otherwise you will burn your tongue (unfortunately I'm talking from experience – it hurts!) and serve either warm or cool. Any spare popcorn can be stored in an airtight container for a few days.

3 tablespoons caster sugar

½ teaspoon ground cinnamon

2 teaspoons cocoa powder, sieved

vegetable or sunflower oil

75g popping corn

PS... *You can add all sorts of flavours to popcorn. Stir some finely grated orange, lemon or lime zest into the sugar or try using vanilla-flavoured sugar.*

If you like savoury popcorn, add some sea salt to the pan instead of the sugar, either plain or flavoured with spices, curry powder or dried herbs. Grated Parmesan mixed with chilli powder is also delicious.

In the mood for a drink? *Surely it has to be an ice-cream soda (laced with a flavoured vodka for a more grown-up version).*

Sticky Citrus Twists

These crisp puff pastry twists with their tangy, sticky coating melt in your mouth as soon as you bite into them. These are a favourite mid-morning treat of mine, but are equally as good with a cup of tea in the afternoon, an espresso after dinner or even with a glass of milk before bed.

* makes about forty
  takes 25-30 minutes to make

Preheat the oven to 200°C/fan 180°C/gas 6.

Cut the pastry in half lengthways, then cut each half into 5mm to 1cm thin strips. Gently twist each strip and lay on to a couple of baking sheets, keeping them slightly apart.

Bake the twists for 8 to 10 minutes, or until they are golden brown. Remove from the oven and leave to cool for about 5 minutes.

While the pastry twists are baking, boil the orange and lemon juice together until you have about 2 tablespoons of juice. Remove from the heat, add the icing sugar and cream and stir until the sugar has dissolved. Pour into a shallow bowl and leave to cool for 5 to 10 minutes to thicken slightly.

Dunk the pastry twists in the glaze until they are coated. Sit on a wire rack, sprinkle with the lemon and orange zest and leave for the glaze to set and any excess to drip off.

375g ready-rolled puff pastry
juice of 1 orange
juice of 1 lemon
150g icing sugar
100ml single cream
finely grated lemon and
  orange zest, to decorate

PS . . . *These are best eaten the day they're made, so if you don't think you will get through them all, just halve the quantities.*

Proper Puds
Classic puddings with a modern twist

You probably don't have a pudding every day of the week, but if you do fancy making one, then you may as well go for it and have a proper pud that is full of naughtiness. Healthy puds have their time and place, but this isn't one of them.

Where do you start with proper puddings? At some time or another, I'm sure you have had an urge for apple pie, treacle tart, a steamed sponge, crumble, bread and butter pudding . . . the list is endless. So, to narrow down the choice, I've decided to make here some of my, and quite possibly some of your, favourite classic puddings, from trifle to sticky toffee.

However, rather than keeping the recipes in their classic form, I have adapted them with a few modern twists so that they stand out from the crowd and create a talking point with whoever you decide to share them with.

They should certainly hit the spot when you're in the mood for a naughty, but extremely nice pudding.

For t
and
gent
boil
stag
wall
Rem
yolk

Pou
a pa
to s
and

Rec
140

To
pea
con
wh
ove
an
the

Co

PS
zes

If
1

I
m

Pa

So f
a cla
the
with
a ta

* se
ta

To r
food
the
I to
com
to a
24c
a fo

Pre

Lir
gre
bea
pap
pas

Pimm's Trifle

Trifle was the best pudding my nana made, the sponge at the bottom almost swimming in booze (sherry, brandy or whisky — whichever bottle was nearest and fullest). This recipe is not very conventional, but I still have a rather boozy base to it and it's a fantastic pudding to serve through summer. After all, summer equals Pimm's, doesn't it?

* **serves six to eight**
  takes about 20 minutes to make

Place the biscotti or cantuccini in the base of a large glass dish (or individual ones if preferred). Pour over the Pimm's and scatter over all the fruits and shredded mint. This can now be left to one side for the biscuits to soak up the Pimm's.

To make the syllabub topping, mix together the icing sugar, sweet wine or sherry and the lemon juice, stirring until the icing sugar has dissolved.

Place the double cream in a large bowl and whisk until it feels like it is just starting to thicken. Add the sweet wine or sherry liquid, whisking while you do so. Continue to whisk until you have wonderful thick, fluffy, boozy cream.

Spoon the cream over the fruits and refrigerate until needed or serve straight away, topped with extra mint leaves and/or toasted almonds.

for the base

1 box of biscotti or cantuccini biscuits (about 250g)

150–200ml Pimm's No. 1 Cup

2 ripe peaches, sliced

2 ripe kiwi fruit, peeled and sliced

2 oranges, segmented

150g raspberries

150g strawberries, halved or quartered

a small bunch of mint leaves, shredded

for the creamy syllabub topping

75g icing sugar

75ml sweet wine or sweet sherry

juice of 1 small lemon

300ml double cream

mint leaves and/or toasted almonds, to garnish

In the mood for a drink? *You probably won't need anything to drink — there's enough in the pudding.*

Pecan Pie with Bourbon

Pecan pie is always delicious, but with an added kick of bourbon it is even nicer. Try this with a scoop of the banana and muscovado ice cream on page 90 for a real treat.

* **serves eight**
  takes about 1 hour to make

First of all, make the pastry, and this really won't take any time at all. Place the flour, sugar and salt in a food processor or mixing bowl and blitz or rub in the butter until it resembles fine breadcrumbs. Add 2 tablespoons of cold water and bind until it just comes together, adding a little more water if it is needed. Knead very lightly on a floured surface to a smooth dough. Roll out and line a 23 to 24cm loose-bottomed tart tin. Prick the base several times with a fork and chill in the fridge for about 20 to 30 minutes.

Preheat the oven to 200°C/fan 180°C fan oven/gas 6.

Line the chilled pastry case with a piece of greaseproof paper and fill with a layer of baking beans or rice. Cook for 15 minutes. Remove the paper, brush the base with a little of the beaten egg and cook for a further 5 minutes until the pastry is just becoming golden.

During the last 5 minutes of cooking the pastry, spread the pecan nuts on a baking tray and toast them in the oven for 5 minutes. Remove and leave to cool slightly.

Reduce the oven temperature to 160°C/fan 140°C/gas 2–3.

Roughly chop half the pecans and mix with all the rest of the filling ingredients, including the whole pecans. Pour and spread into the pastry case. Bake for 20 to 25 minutes, until the centre is just set.

Serve warm with the extra-thick cream, clotted cream or ice cream, or cold with pouring cream.

for the pastry

150g plain flour

1 tablespoon caster sugar

a pinch of salt

100g unsalted butter, chilled and cut into cubes

for the filling

3 large eggs, beaten

250g pecan halves

125g golden syrup

175g soft brown sugar

3 tablespoons bourbon or whisky

40g unsalted butter, melted

1 teaspoon vanilla extract

PS . . . *If you can't be bothered to make your own pastry, use about 300g bought shortcrust pastry and sprinkle over 1 tablespoon of caster sugar while you roll it out.*

Sweet Lemon and
Vanilla Risotto Rice Pudding

This is basically a rice pudding made on the hob, which tends to be creamier than one that is baked because stirring it throughout the cooking time breaks down the starch in the rice grains. Adding a splash of cream before serving finishes it off perfectly, but if you want to be supernaughty, stir in some clotted cream instead.

* **serves two to three**
  takes 30 to 35 minutes to cook

Place the milk in a saucepan. Scrape the vanilla seeds from the pod and place the seeds and pod into the saucepan. Gently heat until the milk almost boils. Remove from the heat.

Melt the butter in a frying pan or saucepan over a low-medium heat and add the sugar and lemon zest. Once it is bubbling and the sugar has dissolved, add the rice. Stir around in the pan for a minute or so until it's coated in the sweet butter.

Gradually add one ladle of the hot milk at a time, stirring almost continuously and allowing the milk to be absorbed before the next ladle is added. The stirring prevents a skin forming on top and breaks down the starch in the rice grains to give a creamier final result. It should take about 30 to 35 minutes for all the milk to be absorbed and the rice to be plump and tender, giving you a delicious thick and creamy risotto.

Remove the pan from the heat and stir in the cream. Taste for sweetness, adding a little extra sugar if you prefer. Spoon into bowls and serve straight away.

800ml full-fat milk

1 vanilla pod, split

20g butter

3 tablespoons caster sugar

grated zest of 1 lemon

125g risotto rice

3 tablespoons double or whipping cream (or a really big spoonful of clotted cream)

PS... *Serve the risotto as it is or with summer berries, grilled plums, peaches or nectarines. For an extra rich finish, add a dollop of your favourite jam.*

In the mood for a drink? *Pick a late harvest Riesling or Eiswein. If it's a German label look out for the sweet 'Beerenauslese' or very sweet 'Trockenbeerenauslese'. Naughty!*

Sticky Ginger Toffee Pudding

Sticky toffee pudding has always been my sister Millie's favourite. She's never been big into puddings, but whenever this is on a menu, she will order it. I have decided to spice up the classic with a storecupboard must-have — stem ginger in syrup.

* serves eight
   takes 30 to 35 minutes to bake

Preheat the oven to 180°C/fan 160°C/gas 4.

Place the dates and tea in a small saucepan and bring to the boil. Cook for 3 to 4 minutes for the dates to soften, and then stir in the bicarbonate of soda.

Cream together the butter and caster sugar before thoroughly mixing in the eggs, flour, stem ginger, mixed spice and date mixture.

Pour into a roughly 22cm square (or similar) buttered baking dish or tin. Bake for 30 to 35 minutes until the top is just firm to touch.

While the pudding is cooking, you can make the sauce by putting the sugar, ginger syrup, butter and cream into a saucepan. Place over a low heat and simmer gently until the sugar has dissolved and the sauce is a light toffee colour.

Serve the pudding with the warm sauce and, if you are feeling really indulgent, a big scoop of vanilla ice cream or clotted cream.

for the pudding

250g dates, stoned and chopped

250ml black tea (not too strong)

1 teaspoon bicarbonate of soda

85g unsalted butter, softened

175g caster sugar

2 large eggs, beaten

175g self-raising flour, sieved

4 balls of stem ginger
   (from a jar), finely chopped

1 teaspoon ground mixed spice

for the sauce

75g light muscovado sugar

4 tablespoons ginger syrup
   from the jar of stem ginger

100g unsalted butter

125ml double cream

PS... *For the best results, try and use medjool dates because they have a lovely natural toffee flavour and sticky texture.*

In the mood for a drink? *Liqueur Muscat or Tokaji Aszu are both big sweet treats with which to tackle this fabulous monster pud.*

Freezing Instructions

If you have an ice-cream machine, then the process is really simple. Follow the manufacturer's instructions and you should have softly frozen ice cream within about 20 minutes.

However, the alternative isn't difficult. Pour the ice cream into a metal or plastic container, cover and freeze for about 1½ hours until the base and sides are becoming frozen. Remove and blitz in a food processor, with an electric hand whisk or energetically by hand with a balloon whisk until smooth. Refreeze, and then repeat a couple more times at hourly intervals so that you end up with a smooth, creamy ice cream rather than one that is full of icy crystals.

Freshly made ice cream can be eaten straight away at the lovely 'just frozen' stage. However, if you are making it ahead of time, keep it well covered in the freezer, where it will set solid. The most important thing then is to move the ice cream from the freezer into the fridge about 20 minutes before you need it, to slightly soften.

Mint Choc-chip

Make the custard base using 1½ teaspoons peppermint extract rather than the vanilla. When cool, stir in 75g chopped plain chocolate or chocolate chips and a little green food colouring if you can't resist. Freeze according to the instructions above.

Strawberry and Marshmallow

Roughly mash 200 to 250g ripe, juicy strawberries and stir into the vanilla custard base with 150g chopped marshmallows. Freeze according to the instructions above.

Banana and Muscovado

Make the vanilla custard base using light or dark muscovado sugar rather than caster sugar. Stir in three ripe, mashed bananas with ½ teaspoon lemon juice and 2 tablespoons banana liqueur for an extra banana kick. Freeze according to the instructions above.

Latte

Make the custard base without the vanilla and stir in 150ml cooled espresso coffee. For the best flavour, use freshly brewed espresso or a strong cafetiere coffee rather than granulated instant. Freeze according to the instructions above.

Summerberry

Take 500g fresh or frozen berries, such as strawberries, raspberries, blueberries and blackberries, and purée with 100g caster or icing sugar in a food processor or blender or by mashing well with a potato masher. Push the purée through a sieve to remove any pips or seeds. Taste for sweetness and add more sugar if it is needed. Stir into the vanilla custard base and freeze according to the instructions on page 90.

Rich Chocolate

Make the vanilla custard base without the vanilla and stir in 175g melted plain chocolate, then freeze according to the instructions on page 90.

Mango and Passion Fruit

Purée the flesh of two large, ripe mangoes with 100g icing sugar in a food processor or blender or by mashing well with a potato masher. Stir in the pulp from four ripe passion fruit (strained if you prefer not to have seeds in your ice cream). Stir into the vanilla custard base and freeze according to the instructions on page 90.

Iced Lemon Sherbet Bonbons

I used to love getting my pocket money on a Saturday morning and spending it on a bag of lemon bonbons. I can't compete with the real thing, but I have made a very refreshing version for when the weather's hot and you fancy a little sweet something to cool you down. These are perfect to keep in your freezer for those sweet somethings.

* makes about twenty bonbons

**takes 20 minutes to make,
plus overnight freezing**

Place the lemon juice in a saucepan and boil until just two-thirds of the liquid is left. Stir in the sugar and syrup until they dissolve. Leave to cool.

Once cold, stir in the sour and double creams until smooth.

Freeze the mixture according to the instructions on page 90, and then leave in the freezer overnight.

Once the lemon sherbet is firm, it can be made into bonbons. This is really easily done. Take a melon baller, a very small ice-cream scoop or a teaspoon measuring spoon, dip into hot water and scoop out balls of the sherbet the size of bonbons. They don't have to be evenly round – the sweets aren't, so don't worry too much about this. Sit the bonbons on a greaseproof paper-lined tray.

Return to the freezer for about 1 hour until firm. They can then be stored in a single layer in an airtight container for you to help yourself to whenever you fancy one.

**100ml freshly squeezed
lemon juice**

175g caster sugar

2 tablespoons golden syrup

200ml sour cream

200ml double cream

Blueberry Cheesecake Parfait

Well, since 'parfait' is the French for 'perfect', need I say any more? The parfait can be made in a cake or bread tin or in individual moulds such as metal rings, dariole moulds, ramekins, cups or even old plastic yoghurt pots.

* serves at least eight
takes about 30 to 40 minutes to make, plus freezing overnight

To make the blueberry compote, stir the cornflour into the lemon juice in a small saucepan. Add the blueberries and icing sugar and place over a low-medium heat. Cook until the blueberries are bursting and their juices run, giving you a rich purple sauce. Remove from the heat and leave to cool.

To make the base, mix together the crumbled biscuits and butter. Line the base and sides of a round 20cm springform cake tin, a bread tin, a terrine or eight individual moulds with greaseproof paper and press the biscuit mixture firmly into the base.

To make the cheesecake, beat together the mascarpone and custard until smooth. Boil the sugar, lemon zest and 75ml water for 5 minutes to create a lemon-flavoured syrup. Remove the lemon zest.

Whisk the egg whites to soft peaks, and then slowly pour in the hot sugar syrup, whisking as you do so. Continue to whisk until the 'meringue' is at room temperature, and then fold it into the creamy custard mixture until smooth. Now, swirl in the blueberry compote and pour on top of the biscuit base. Spread the surface flat and place in the freezer overnight, or longer.

When it comes to serving, remove from the freezer, briefly dip the mould in hot water or slide a hot knife around the inside, and turn out on to a plate. For a large parfait, slice into portions using a hot knife, and then place in the fridge for about 1 hour. Individual parfaits can go straight on to plates to be kept in the fridge for the same amount of time, to give you a chilled mousse-like dessert, rather than an icy frozen cheesecake to tuck into.

for the blueberry compote
1 teaspoon cornflour
juice of 1 lemon
250g blueberries
3 tablespoons icing sugar

for the base
200g digestive biscuits,
crushed to fine crumbs
75g butter, melted

for the cheesecake
250g mascarpone cheese
225ml ready-made or
home-made custard
125g caster sugar
4 strips of lemon zest
2 large egg whites

PS...*Blackcurrants, blackberries or raspberries are all very tasty alternatives to blueberries.*

Rhubarb and Custard Iced Lollies

I have always loved the double act combination of rhubarb and custard — maybe something to do with the fact that it's one of my favourite childhood cartoons (I'm showing my age now). These look fantastic — resembling a sophisticated rocket iced lolly (oops, showing my age again). They are best made in tall shot glasses and taste amazing. Keep them in your freezer to impress your friends with when the mood for reliving your childhood days grabs you.

* **makes about six**

   takes 20 minutes to make,
   plus 4 to 5 hours freezing time

To make the rhubarb layer, place the rhubarb in a saucepan with the sugar and cook over a gentle heat until it has softened to a purée consistency. Stir in the ginger syrup, if using, transfer to a blender or food processor and blitz to a smooth purée. Leave to cool, and then pour into the glasses or moulds. The purée needs to come halfway up the glasses or moulds. Freeze for about 2 hours until firm.

For the custard layer, lightly whip the double cream, and then stir in the custard, vanilla extract or seeds and icing sugar. Spoon or pour on top of the frozen rhubarb layer. Place a lolly stick in each one and freeze for 2 to 3 hours. If you can't get lolly sticks, neatly trim long wooden skewers into equal lengths, without leaving any splintery ends, and place three together in each lolly. You could also stick in small metal teaspoons.

Remove the lollies from the freezer 15 to 20 minutes before you need them to make it easier to pull them out of their glasses or moulds. If you can't wait that long, dip them into warm water.

for the rhubarb layer
250g rhubarb,
   trimmed and finely sliced
100g caster sugar
1 tablespoon ginger syrup from
   a jar of stem ginger (optional)

for the custard layer
75ml double cream
150ml bought ready-made custard
¼ teaspoon vanilla extract, or
   scraped seeds of 1 vanilla pod
1 tablespoon icing sugar, sifted

you will also need
tall double shot glasses or lolly moulds
wooden lolly sticks, wooden
   skewers or teaspoons

PS . . . *Rhubarb and custard is a classic combination, but any fruit purée will work with the custard, so have a play around with different flavours. You can even speed up the process by using tinned fruit in syrup, bought fruit purées or sauces.*

Piña Colada Sundae

If a piña colada cocktail is good enough for Delboy, then an edible version is certainly worthy of making its way into this book.

* **makes about six sundaes**

   **takes about 30 minutes to make,
   plus freezing time**

To make the pineapple and rum sorbet, dissolve the sugar in 75ml water in a small saucepan, and then simmer for 2 minutes. Leave to cool.

Blitz the pineapple flesh in a blender for at least a couple of minutes so you have a super smooth liquid purée. Add the cooled sugar syrup, lime juice and rum. Blitz to combine. Freeze according the instructions on page 90.

To make the coconut ice cream, bring the coconut milk and desiccated coconut to the boil in a non-stick saucepan. Beat together the egg yolks and caster sugar until they are thick and creamy. Stir in the coconut milk, and then pour everything back into the saucepan. Stir continuously over a low heat for a few minutes until it just starts to thicken slightly. Remove the pan from the heat and leave to cool. Once cool, you can either strain through a sieve to give you a smooth ice cream or leave it as it is, keeping in the desiccated coconut. I prefer a smooth ice cream, but it's totally up to you. Stir in the double cream and freeze according to the instructions on page 90.

To make up the sundaes, get some sundae glasses and layer up a couple of scoops each of the sorbet and ice cream with pieces of the fresh pineapple, sliced kiwi, sprinklings of toasted coconut and whipped cream. Finish with a good glug of Malibu, a maraschino cherry, a paper umbrella and any other decoration that takes your fancy!

for the pineapple and rum sorbet

100g caster sugar

1 medium-large ripe, sweet pineapple, peeled, core removed and roughly chopped

juice of 1 lime

3 tablespoons white rum

for the coconut ice cream

400ml tin of coconut milk

50g desiccated coconut

3 large egg yolks

200g caster sugar

200ml double cream

to make up the sundaes

chunks of ripe pineapple

2 kiwi fruit, peeled and sliced

toasted thinly sliced fresh or desiccated coconut (see PS...)

whipped cream

Malibu (coconut liqueur)

maraschino cherries, paper cocktail umbrellas or other over-the-top decorations if you're feeling flamboyant

PS...*To toast the coconut, preheat the oven to 160°C/fan 140°C/gas mark 2–3. Bake the coconut for 10 to 15 minutes, turning a couple of times, until golden.*

In the Mood for Some
Comfort

Too much partying, you're overworked, feeling under the weather, love life stinks, broke, cold, lonely or just plain fed up – phew! The list is endless, but whatever it is, feeding ourselves warming, soothing food seems to provide at least temporary relief every time.

I was asking some of my friends about when they would be in the mood for comfort food and I was given the answer I expected almost every time: 'When I have a hangover.' I wasn't really surprised. It goes without saying that when you wake up with a hangover all you seem to want is filling carbohydrates and anything bad for you. These foods have a relaxing and comforting effect on your brain, which makes us crave them. After drinking alcohol, blood-sugar levels tend to be low, which also puts us in the mood for a fairly instant energy boost from carbs and sugar. It's certainly not the healthiest way of treating a hangover, but I can't say I know many people who are in the mood for a healthy breakfast after a night on the tiles!

It's not just hangovers that can put you in the mood for comfort food. A lot of the time, the mood strikes during the cold winter months. I guess it's because the days are shorter, the nights darker and there is something so comforting about closing the curtains and

Cream of Tomato Soup with Croque-monsieur Croutons

Heinz tomato soup is the ultimate 'poorly' food. For me, it brings back memories of when my mum gave it to me if I was off school: mine with a swirl of cream on top and hers with a dash of sherry. I won't attempt to better the soup, but here's a great recipe for croque-monsieur croutons to add extra comfort value.

* serves four
takes 10 minutes to make

Heat the soup until it is steaming but not boiling.

To make the croutons, butter both sides of all the bread slices and scatter half of the cheese over two of them. Lay the ham on top, and then scatter over the remaining cheese. Add a twist of black pepper, top with the remaining bread and press down firmly.

Heat a good drizzle of olive oil in a frying pan over a medium heat. Place the sandwiches in the pan (you may need to do one at a time, depending on the size of your pan). Leave for 1 to 2 minutes until the base is golden and the cheese is starting to melt. Turn over and cook for a further minute, or until golden.

Remove from the pan and leave to cool for 5 minutes to make the croque-monsieurs easier to cut into cubes.

Ladle the soup into bowls and add a swirl of cream and/or sherry. Scatter over the croutons and enjoy straight away.

for the soup
Heinz tomato soup
(as much as you fancy)
cream and/or sherry

for the croutons
4 slices of white bread
butter
100g Gruyère cheese,
finely grated
2 thin slices of ham
freshly ground black pepper
olive oil

PS...*The croque-monsieurs can be served cut into fingers rather than croutons if you like.*

For a little kick, I occasionally like to spread Dijon mustard over the bread before I add the cheese.

Cauliflower Cheese Soup

Just imagine wrapping your hands around a steaming hot bowl of this creamy and filling soup. Its mild flavour is great if you are feeling a little delicate and after a bowl of this, your body will be full of goodness from top to toe. Crusty fresh bread to dip in is a must, but if you want to be a bit posh, then try the crispy rosemary and Parmesan croutons — they are delicious (see PS . . .).

* serves six
takes about 45 minutes to make

Melt the butter in a large saucepan. Add the onion and cook until it is softened but not coloured. Stir in the garlic, bay leaf, cauliflower and potato. Reduce the heat, cover with a lid and leave to cook for 10 minutes, stirring occasionally. Make sure the vegetables don't brown and if they are sticking, then add a splash of water to the pan.

Remove the lid and pour in the milk and 700ml of the stock. Simmer for 15 minutes, until the cauliflower and potato are tender and beginning to break up.

Remove from the heat and take out the bay leaf. Cool slightly, and then blitz in a food processor or blender until totally smooth. You'll probably have to do this in two batches. Return the soup to the pan and stir in the mustard and Cheddar until the cheese has melted. Season with salt and pepper.

Have a taste and add extra mustard or cheese for a stronger flavour if you prefer. The remaining 200ml of stock can be added if the soup seems particularly thick. Serve in deep bowls or big mugs and dunk in crusty bread or scatter with croutons.

50g butter

1 onion, chopped

2 cloves of garlic, crushed

1 bay leaf

1 large cauliflower, broken into small florets (you need about 800g florets)

1 baking potato, peeled and chopped

500ml milk

700–900ml vegetable stock

1 teaspoon English mustard

200g extra mature Cheddar cheese, grated

sea salt and freshly ground black pepper

PS . . . *To make some really tasty, crunchy rosemary and Parmesan croutons, cut two thick slices of white bread into 1cm cubes. Heat 3 tablespoons of rosemary-infused oil in a frying pan and fry the bread until golden all over. Tip on to a baking sheet and scatter with 50g finely grated Parmesan. Place in a hot oven until the Parmesan has melted on to the croutons. Scatter over the soup. If you haven't any rosemary oil, plain olive oil or another flavoured oil, say garlic or basil, can be used.*

Creamy Sautéed Mushrooms on Toast

This creamy mushrooms on toast is wonderfully quick and simple to make. Not only that, it's good for you too. The amount of mushrooms used here contributes to just over two portions of your 'five a day', and they're high in B vitamins, which collectively may help to relieve stress, depression and fatigue. Try and use a selection of mushrooms if you can: chestnut, portobello, flat or wild ones. But if all you can get is the common button mushroom, then that's just fine too.

* serves one
  takes 10 minutes to make

Warm the butter and a trickle of olive oil in a pan and once the butter bubbles, toss in the mushrooms. Toss around until they are beginning to colour slightly without going soggy.

Squeeze in a little lemon juice, add the parsley and a splash of cream. Bubble for the cream to thicken a little. Season with salt and pepper and spoon, straight away, over the hot toasted bread.

a knob of butter

olive oil

about 225g mushrooms (whatever you like), cut into bite-sized pieces if large

a squeeze of lemon

a small handful of chopped parsley

a splash of double cream

sea salt and freshly ground black pepper

thick slices of toasted bread

PS...*For additional flavour, add a clove of garlic to the pan when the mushrooms go in. Or for a meaty element, fry cubes of bacon or pancetta in the pan until crisp before adding the mushrooms.*

Fish Pie with a Sweet Potato Topping

If I am feeling a little under the weather, I often crave a good old-fashioned fish pie. I always think of it as one of those foods that would get me better when I was younger — and still do now. The problem is that it can take a while to prepare, so I have put together a recipe that isn't at all complicated or time consuming, without compromising on flavour. I have used sweet potato for the topping, but you can just as easily use white potatoes if you prefer.

* **serves four**
  takes up to 1 hour to make

Preheat the oven to 180°C/fan 160°C/gas 4.

Melt the butter in a large saucepan. Add the spring onions and cook until they are softened. Stir in the flour, cooking for about 30 seconds before gradually adding the milk. Bring to a simmer, cooking for a couple of minutes until you have a smooth, thick sauce. Stir in the fish, prawns, smoked salmon, dill or parsley, lemon zest and a squeeze of lemon juice and season lightly with salt and pepper. Once the sauce is bubbling and the cod is starting to flake a little, remove from the heat.

Spoon into one large (1.5 to 1.8 litre) pie dish or four individual dishes and leave to cool while you prepare the topping.

To make the topping, coarsely grate the sweet potato. Place in a clean tea towel and squeeze out the excess water over the sink. Melt the butter in a saucepan and add the grated potato. Stir over a medium heat for a couple of minutes until the potato is coated in the butter and starting to soften.

Scatter the potato over the top of the pie, leaving a rough topping rather than pressing it down. Sprinkle over the grated cheese.

Sit on a baking tray and bake for 30 minutes, until the top is golden and the filling is starting to bubble over the edges. Serve the pie just as it is or with a healthy portion of peas.

for the pie

50g butter

1 bunch of spring onions, sliced

50g plain flour

400ml milk

500g cod, coley, haddock or halibut fillets, skinned and cut into chunks

200g cooked tiger prawns

150g smoked salmon, cut into strips

1 tablespoon chopped dill or parsley

grated zest of 1 lemon

a squeeze of lemon

sea salt and freshly ground black pepper

for the topping

700g sweet potatoes, peeled

40g butter

50g mature Cheddar cheese, grated

Lucozade and Orange Jelly

Tucking into one of these when you're suffering from a cold and a bad throat should perk you up in no time at all. The throat-soothing jelly contains loads of glucose from the Lucozade and vitamin C from the oranges.

* makes four

**takes 10 minutes to make,
plus about 2 hours setting time**

Heat the orange juice either in a small saucepan or in the microwave. Cut the jelly into pieces (I find scissors far easier than using a knife) and stir into the hot juice until the jelly has dissolved completely.

Stir in the Lucozade, and then pour into one large dish or four individual dishes or glasses.

Chill in the fridge for a couple of hours until the jelly has set. Serve with a good dose of cream and some halved grapes on top.

**200ml orange juice
(freshly squeezed if possible)**
125g packet of orange jelly
375ml original Lucozade
cream, to serve
**1 small bunch of grapes,
to serve**

Roast Chicken for Two . . . in One Pan

So, there are just the two of you and all you fancy is a comforting roast dinner, but just the thought of the numerous pots and pans and immense effort puts you off. Well, this could be your saviour.

* serves two
takes about 1½ hours to make

Preheat the oven to 200°C/fan 180°C/gas 6.

Cook the potatoes in boiling salted water for 10 to 12 minutes until they are almost cooked through. Drain and cool for a few minutes.

Rub the garlic all over the chicken, then place a couple of cloves inside and the others at one end of a large roasting tray. Add the rosemary and a drizzle of olive oil to the tray with the garlic. Quarter the lemon and rub all over the chicken skin, squeezing lightly to release some juice. Place a couple of the quarters inside the chicken and the other two in the roasting tray with the garlic and rosemary. Sit the chicken on top of the flavourings and place the shallots next to the chicken. Drizzle both with a little olive oil and season with salt and pepper.

Crush each potato lightly so they are just holding their shape, but are crumbling at the edges. Add to the tray and toss gently in 2 tablespoons of olive oil. Roast for 1 hour, or until the chicken is golden and the potatoes crisp. Baste the chicken a couple of times, turning the shallots and potatoes at the same time.

When cooked, remove the chicken, shallots and potatoes from the tray and leave to rest in a warm place. Throw out the garlic, rosemary and lemon. Place the roasting tray on the hob over a high heat. Pour in the sherry and honey and allow to bubble . Scrape the sticky residue from the bottom of the pan. Add the chicken stock and let it boil for a couple of minutes before adding the peas. Once it returns to the boil, cook for 2 to 3 minutes before finally stirring in the cream and some seasoning.

Carve the chicken and serve on warm plates with the shallots and crunchy potatoes, and pour the sherry gravy all over.

500g new potatoes

4 cloves of garlic, peeled and flattened with the back of a knife

1 small (approximately 1kg) free-range or organic chicken

a sprig of fresh rosemary

olive oil

1 lemon

10 shallots, peeled and left whole

sea salt and freshly ground black pepper

1 small glass of sherry

1 tablespoon runny honey

200ml chicken stock

150g frozen peas

a splash of double cream

In the mood for a drink?
Chicken rocks with red or white — a great choice for white is Chardonnay with some body from Burgundy in France or you could go for a lighter style of red such as Pinot Noir.

Chianti Baked Meatballs

This recipe first came about when my husband Phil was training to do the London marathon. He could eat for England after a long run on a Sunday afternoon and rather than attempting the running, I would be the good wife and prepare this hearty delight. Serve with rigatoni, penne or spaghetti or some chunks of potato mixed with rosemary and olive oil and baked in the oven alongside the meatballs.

*** serves four
(or two if you have a marathon runner to feed!)
takes about 1 hour to make**

Preheat the oven to 220°C/fan 200°C/gas 7.

To make the meatballs, all you need to do is mix everything together really well (this is much easier using your hands). Now, using wet hands, divide the mixture into about twelve large or twenty small balls (giving three large or five small meatballs per portion).

Lightly toss the meatballs in the olive oil in an ovenproof sauté pan or a roasting tray. Choose one that is just big enough to fit the meatballs, but not so small that they are squashed together or so big that the liquid evaporates too quickly, leaving less sauce.

Bake the meatballs for 10 minutes, and then pour over the Chianti, turning the meatballs so they are coated in the red wine. There may be some residue in the pan from the meat. This is fine, just stir it into the wine and it will all cook together to give a lovely flavour.

Return to the oven for 10 minutes, and then stir in the chopped tomatoes, sugar and basil. Cook for a further 20 to 25 minutes until the sauce is bubbling and thickened.

Serve straight away with some pasta or baked rosemary potatoes.

for the meatballs

500g minced beef

1 onion, very finely chopped

2 cloves of garlic, crushed

50g stoned black olives, chopped

50g breadcrumbs

**25g finely grated
Parmesan cheese**

1 lightly beaten egg

1 teaspoon paprika

1 long red chilli, finely chopped

2–3 tablespoons chopped parsley

**sea salt and freshly ground
black pepper**

for the sauce

2 tablespoons olive oil

250ml Chianti red wine

**2 x 400g tins of chopped
tomatoes**

2 teaspoons caster sugar

a large handful of chopped basil

In the mood for a drink? *It has to be Chianti, of course.*

Cheese, Onion and Potato Pie

Sometimes you just need comfort food in the stodgiest form. This isn't really a pie, but more of a bake and reminds me of a fantastic one I used to love at primary school. I like to make it with Cheddar, but you can use almost any cheese you like – grated or crumbled. Stilton or Gruyère are also favourites of mine, but only when I'm in the mood for a stronger flavour.

*** serves two generously
takes about 45 minutes to make**

Preheat the oven to 200°C/fan 180°C/gas 6.

Cook the potatoes in boiling salted water for 15 to 20 minutes until tender.

While the potatoes are cooking, melt the butter in a pan and gently sauté the onion until lightly golden and sweet. This will take about 10 minutes. Add the milk to the pan and heat until almost boiling.

Drain the potatoes and return back to the pan. Mash really well with a potato masher, and then beat in the milk and onion, three-quarters of the cheese, the mustard and some seasoning.

Transfer to a buttered ovenproof dish, scatter over the remaining cheese and lay the tomato slices on top.

Bake for 20 to 25 minutes until the top is bubbling and lightly golden.

750g potatoes, peeled and quartered

40g butter

1 large onion, thinly sliced

100ml milk

200g mature Cheddar, Double Gloucester or Red Leicester cheese, grated

1 teaspoon wholegrain or English mustard

sea salt and freshly ground black pepper

2–3 tomatoes, sliced

PS... *All sorts of flavours can be added to the pie:*
* *Cubes of ham, cooked crispy bacon, sliced salami or chorizo.*
* *Flakes of smoked mackerel or hot smoked salmon.*
* *Sautéed mushrooms or red pepper.*
* *Chopped herbs, such as thyme, basil or chives.*

In the mood for a drink? *Track down a bottle of Pinot Gris, whose generous body and texture will match the weight of the dish without overwhelming the flavour. A simple alternative is Chardonnay.*

Extremely Simple Beef and Ale Casserole with Horseradish Dumplings

The best thing about this casserole is that there is virtually nothing to do. Fry a few onions, add the rest of the casserole ingredients and let it cook while you do absolutely nothing. The only bit of effort required is to throw together the fluffy dumplings.

* serves four
takes 2 hours to cook

Preheat the oven to 160°C/fan 140°C/gas 2–3.

Heat the oil in a large casserole and add the onion. Cook until starting to colour.

Toss the beef in the flour and season well with salt and pepper. This can either be done in a bowl or, to make the job really easy, toss together in a large freezer bag. Add to the casserole with all of the remaining casserole ingredients. Stir to mix everything together, and then bring to the boil. Cover with a lid and place in the oven for 1½ hours.

When the casserole is close to the end of the cooking time, you can make the dumplings. Place the flour, breadcrumbs and butter in a food processor and blitz to a crumb consistency. Add the horseradish, thyme, egg and seasoning. Briefly blitz until the mixture forms a fairly moist dough. Using floured hands, shape the dough into eight balls.

After 1½ hours, remove the casserole from the oven and sit the dumplings on top of the meat. Sprinkle their tops with a few flakes of salt and return the casserole to the oven for a further 30 minutes, without the lid this time. Serve the casserole just as it is or with some buttery cabbage or curly kale.

PS . . . *If you want to transform the casserole into a pie, bake for 1½ hours, transfer to a pie dish and, instead of dumplings, top with ready-rolled puff or shortcrust pastry. Brush with a little milk or egg yolk and bake at 200°C/fan 180°C/gas 6 for 25 to 30 minutes until golden.*

for the casserole

2 tablespoons vegetable oil

2 large onions, thickly sliced

750g braising steak, cut into 2–3cm cubes

3 tablespoons plain flour

sea salt and freshly ground black pepper

2 sticks of celery, sliced

2 carrots, peeled and sliced

2 tablespoons demerara sugar

2 tablespoons balsamic vinegar

2 teaspoons Worcestershire sauce

2 tablespoons tomato purée

500ml ale

for the dumplings

75g self-raising flour, plus extra for dusting

75g fresh white breadcrumbs

75g butter, cubed

1 tablespoon hot horseradish sauce

2 teaspoons thyme leaves

1 large egg, lightly beaten

sea salt and freshly ground black pepper

Saucy Banana and Caramel Pudding

When you want a little comfort from a hot, sticky pudding, then you really must give this a go. It's so quick and easy to throw together and smells amazing when it's cooking.

* **serves six**
  takes 1 hour to make

Preheat the oven to 180°C/fan 160°C/gas 4.

Sift the flour, baking powder and mixed spice or cinnamon into a bowl, and then beat in the sugar, mashed banana, egg, milk and butter until well combined.

Pour into a buttered 1.5 to 2 litre ovenproof dish or six individual dishes (about 300ml to 400ml each).

To make the sauce, place the golden syrup, muscovado sugar and 250ml water in a small pan over a medium heat. Stir until dissolved and bring to the boil. Pour immediately over the top of the pudding and place in the oven for 30 to 40 minutes until golden and just firm in the centre when lightly pressed.

Leave to cool for a few minutes and serve just as it is or with ice cream, cream or crème fraîche.

for the pudding

125g plain flour

1 tablespoon baking powder

½ teaspoon mixed spice or cinnamon

125g light muscovado sugar

2 ripe bananas, mashed

1 large egg, beaten

200ml milk

75g unsalted butter, melted

for the sauce

4 tablespoons golden syrup

125g light muscovado sugar

PS . . . *You can add 75g chopped walnuts, pecans and/or sultanas or raisins into the pudding mixture before baking.*

Overworked and Underfed
Calming suppers for stressful work days

You feel so hard done by and totally fed up when you've had a busy, stressful day at work and not stopped long enough to fill up on body fuel. By the time you get home, you are exhausted and in total need of some satisfying and tasty food.

Obviously, there are times when I just need food instantly and for those times I will do a recipe from the In the Mood for Being Lazy chapter (see page 143). However, there is something very relaxing and stress-busting about spending some time in the kitchen. Just the process of cooking can give comfort. You come home after a hard day and calm down, taking time out from the rest of the world to prepare dinner. It's a great way to switch off from the day and just concentrate on the job in hand.

There are certain foods that you crave at times like this, usually foods that are full of flavour and wonderfully satisfying. You don't mind if they're not the healthiest of foods (after all, you deserve a treat after the day you've just had) but you don't necessarily want to go full on naughty. It's about getting the right balance — food to satisfy your body and mind.

I find a risotto is the perfect dish when I'm tired and stressed, but very hungry. Yes, I know it takes a while to cook and you have to stand and stir for some time, but I find having a glass of wine on the go and flicking through a magazine or having a gossip with someone on the phone makes the time go very pleasantly.

Many people turn to pasta when in need of something quick and comforting. Not only does pasta take no time at all to cook and doesn't require much effort to create a delicious meal, but it has the added bonus that the starches in the pasta help you become relaxed and sleepy. Have a look at the recipes from the Pasta Pronto section on page 180 for more sauces to serve with pasta.

'Oh So Simple' Chicken, Leek and Ham Pies

This is for those times when you rush through the supermarket on your way home and get a whiff of roasting chickens from the rotisserie counter. Perhaps you don't usually get one because you can't be bothered to do all the trimmings — roast potatoes, gravy and veggies — or because you feel like something more substantial than a hot chicken sandwich or salad. So why not make use of one to fill a puff pastry-topped pie that will take no time at all to put together.

* **makes one large or four individual pies**
  takes about 35 minutes to make

Preheat the oven to 200°C/fan 180°C/gas 6.

Melt the butter in a large saucepan and gently cook the leek and thyme leaves until the leek has softened. Increase the heat, pour in the sherry and cream and bubble for a couple of minutes to thicken a little.

Take the chicken meat off the bone and tear into chunks or strips. Add to the pan with the ham, mustard and chicken stock and season with salt and pepper. Bring to a simmer and cook for a few minutes until the sauce has thickened slightly.

Spoon into one large or four individual pie dishes. Brush the rim of each dish with the egg wash, cut the pastry into four (or leave whole if you are doing one large pie) and sit on top. Press the edges down well to seal and trim off any excess pastry. Cut a small slit in the top to let any steam escape and brush with the egg wash.

Bake for 15 minutes until the tops are golden and the sauce begins to ooze out of the dishes. Serve straight away.

25g butter

2 small-medium leeks, thinly sliced

1 teaspoon thyme leaves

100ml sherry or white wine

200ml double cream

1 large ready-roasted chicken

150–200g piece of ham, cut into bite-sized chunks

2 teaspoons Dijon mustard

100ml chicken stock

sea salt and freshly ground black pepper

1 egg yolk mixed with 1 tablespoon milk, to glaze

375g ready-rolled puff pastry

PS . . . *If you can't get a ready-roasted chicken, then you can cook chopped breast or leg meat in the pan before adding the leek.*

Leek, Dolcelatte and Pancetta Risotto

It does take a bit of time to stir a risotto, but the end result is worth it. It's also amazing how the relaxed process of making a risotto is so comforting. Pick up the phone, or a glass of wine and a magazine, and you'll be set up for about twenty minutes of stirring.

* **serves four**

   takes 35 to 40 minutes to make (most of it is taken up with relaxed stirring though)

Heat the olive oil and butter in a deep, heavy-based frying pan or sauté pan. Gently cook the leek and garlic until soft but not colouring at all. This should take about 10 minutes.

Add the rice and thyme or rosemary and stir for about a minute until the rice looks slightly translucent. Pour in the wine and stir continuously until it has cooked into the rice. Add a good ladle of hot stock and season with salt and pepper. Turn the heat down so the risotto is simmering gently and keep adding ladles of stock as it cooks into the rice, stirring and moving the rice around in the pan.

After about 15 to 20 minutes, the rice should be soft but still with a bit of bite left in it. The texture of the risotto should be thick and creamy, but not too loose. Add extra stock or hot water if necessary.

While the risotto is cooking, slowly fry the pancetta until it is golden and crispy and keep warm.

Remove the cooked risotto from the heat, fish out the thyme or rosemary sprigs and gently stir in the dolcelatte to give a velvety texture. Add extra stock if the risotto seems particularly thick. Spoon into bowls and scatter with the pancetta.

2 tablespoons olive oil

a good knob of butter

2 large leeks, sliced

2 cloves of garlic, crushed

350g risotto rice

a couple of sprigs of thyme or rosemary

1 large glass of dry white wine

1–1.2 litres hot vegetable or chicken stock

sea salt and freshly ground black pepper

150g pancetta or smoky bacon cubes

225g creamy Dolcelatte cheese, cut into cubes

PS... *For a vegetarian risotto, the pancetta can be swapped for some walnut pieces. Toast them in a dry frying pan first to get the best flavour out of them, then scatter over the top just before serving.*

In the mood for a drink? *There's some robust flavours here, so go for an older red such as a Gran Reserva Rioja from Spain.*

Roasted Balsamic Onion and Cherry Tomato Lasagnes

Some lasagnes can be hard work to make, but this isn't at all. I like to make the lasagne in individual dishes so I can freeze a couple before baking and have them ready for when the mood arises again.

* serves four

takes about 1¼ hours to make (most of that is cooking time though – the perfect opportunity for you to put your feet up)

Preheat the oven to 200°C/fan 180°C/gas 6.

Cut each onion into about six wedges. Put in a roasting tray and toss in the olive oil. Roast for 20 to 25 minutes, turning a couple of times, until they become golden. Add the tomatoes, balsamic vinegar and three tablespoons of water (or white wine if you have some open) to the tray and roast for a further 10 minutes. Remove the tray from the oven and gently stir in the olives, basil and seasoning.

In a bowl, mix together the cream or milk, ricotta, half of the Parmesan and some seasoning. Spoon a third of the roasted onion and tomato mixture into the base of four ovenproof dishes and top with a sheet of lasagne. Repeat two more times, finishing with a sheet of lasagne. Spread the ricotta mixture over the top and scatter over the remaining Parmesan.

Bake for 30 minutes until the lasagnes are golden and cooked through. Serve straight away with the very good garlic bread opposite, for extra comfort value.

4 medium-large red onions

2 tablespoons olive oil

1kg cherry tomatoes

1 tablespoon balsamic vinegar

a large handful of stoned black olives, halved

a large handful of basil, roughly chopped

sea salt and freshly ground black pepper

150ml single cream or milk

250g ricotta cheese

75g grated Parmesan cheese

12 sheets of fresh lasagne

PS . . . *If you can't get hold of fresh lasagne, then cook some dried lasagne sheets in boiling salted water for 5 minutes, drain and use as above. Even if the packet states that the lasagne doesn't need precooking, I have found it's best to do so for this recipe otherwise it can be quite dry once cooked.*

In the mood for a drink? *Italian red hits the spot. Try a Chianti (made from mainly Sangiovese grapes) or Montelpulciano d'Abruzzo.*

Very Good Garlic Bread

For me, when I am feeling really overworked and underfed, there is nothing better than munching on crisp garlic bread with a melt in-the-mouth centre oozing garlicky butter. I could eat it with anything, but it is really lovely with the leek, dolcelatte and pancetta risotto on page 136 or the roasted balsamic onion and cherry tomato lasagnes opposite.

* **makes enough for two to four
  (I could eat the whole thing alone though)**

  takes 20 minutes to cook

Preheat the oven to 220°C/fan 200°C/gas 7.

Mix together the butter, garlic, parsley and a good pinch of salt.

Cut deep slashes into the baguette, trying not to cut right through. Spread the garlic butter into the slashes, and then wrap loosely in foil.

Cook for 15 minutes, and then open up the foil and cook for a further 5 minutes to crisp up the outside.

Now all you need to do is tear the baguette into pieces and munch away.

100g butter, softened

3 plump cloves of garlic, crushed

a small handful of parsley, finely chopped

sea salt

a small baguette (about 30cm long)

PS . . . *Another of my favourite recipes is to add 50g coarsely grated Parmesan cheese and a pinch of paprika to the butter instead of the garlic and parsley.*

For herb and garlic bread, add an additional handful of chopped mixed basil, chives, tarragon and thyme to the butter.

Berry and Ginger Crumbles

Yum — a juicy fruit crumble with a crisp, nutty topping that can be made when you are feeling hard done by at any time of the year. This one is really simple to make and, before you know it, the juices will be bubbling over the edge of your dish. For the ultimate comfort factor, you have to serve it with lashings of custard.

* **makes two generous crumbles**
  takes about 20 to 25 minutes to make

Preheat the oven to 180°C/fan 160°C/gas 4.

Place the berries in a sieve over a bowl to drain away any excess juices.

To make the topping, lightly rub together the butter, flour and salt, and then stir in the sugar, oats and flaked almonds. Try not to over handle the mixture; it wants to be fairly chunky and crumbly.

Now back to the filling. Mix the drained fruits with the ginger, orange zest and sugar. Spoon into two individual ovenproof dishes (or one larger dish to share) and pile the crumble mixture on top. Scatter over a little more demerara sugar and sit the dishes on a baking tray.

Bake for 20 to 25 minutes or until the topping is crisp and golden and the fruity juices are just starting to ooze out of the dishes.

Serve just as they are or with your favourite creamy comfort (mine is custard, but thick cream, ice cream or crème fraîche are all good).

for the fruit

350g frozen mixed berries, defrosted

1 ball of stem ginger (from a jar), finely chopped

grated zest of 1 orange

4 tablespoons caster sugar

for the topping

50g unsalted butter, softened

75g plain flour

a pinch of sea salt

40g demerara sugar, plus extra for sprinkling

20g rolled oats

20g flaked almonds, crushed lightly in your hands

PS... *You don't have to stick to frozen fruits for this, they are just a very convenient ingredient, especially when many fruits are out of season. You can of course use any fresh fruit or berries you like, altering the amount of sugar depending on what you choose.*

In the Mood for Being *Lazy*

Just where does time go? I know I'm not the only one that races around all week — finishing work later than planned, getting caught up in traffic, stuck on a tube, going out for a drink after work (and staying for just one more), a gym class to get to, a quick bit of retail therapy before the shops shut . . . I could go on. Basically, it's at times like this that when you finally get home, you're in such a lazy mood you can't be bothered to do much cooking, but still want something really tasty and satisfying to eat.

It would be so easy to pick up the phone and order a takeaway, cook a ready meal in the microwave or have beans on toast (again). However, just because you're feeling lazy doesn't mean you have to compromise. You can still tuck into some proper, home-cooked food with minimum effort, from the shopping and preparation to the cooking, and even the washing-up. You'll find that if you turn to ready-made convenience foods (baked beans on toast doesn't count here — it's one of my favourites and is actually quite nutritious) you will feel more tired and lazy from the lack of nutrients. Cooking for yourself makes you feel much more healthy, far less lazy and certainly lifts your mood.

What about those times when you're home alone and cooking for one? To many people, it seems like a boring chore, but I like to think of it as a time when you can be totally selfish and cook what you like without having to please anyone else. Provided nothing takes too long to make, I don't mind being in the kitchen on my own.

What if you're cooking for more than just one? There are often occasions when I have invited friends round for dinner or my hungry hubby Phil and I want to eat something that gives maximum satisfaction with minimum effort, usually midweek when we're both working hard. I thought I'd give you a little inspiration with some quick-to-prepare recipes using simple ingredients that only require a dash round the supermarket or shops. It's always a good idea to have a few ideas up your sleeve so you don't get home with a handful of ingredients you don't actually know what you're going to do with.

There are times, however, when the very thought of going shopping for food really isn't what you are in the mood for. Maybe you're all chilled out after watching a film, revising, doing some DIY or have just arrived home after a few drinks and the hunger pangs strike. You'll be amazed at how much you can magically put together with ingredients that are already sitting in your kitchen. And if they aren't, read through my shopping list on page 169 so you can stock up to make my Emergency Zone recipes at those times of ultimate laziness.

And on the subject of essential ingredients, I bet you always have a bag of pasta in your cupboard? Yep – thought so. I think pasta is the ultimate food for when you are in the mood for being lazy. It's quick to cook and you can make some deliciously simple flavours and sauces to go with it. Read on to find out what I've come up with to make our lives that little bit easier and your lazy mood meals tastier.

Home Alone
Cooking for one a chore? Think again

So you're home alone, hungry and tired. Forget the usual thoughts that cooking for one is a chore, boring and depressing. Just remind yourself that it's a perfect opportunity to be completely selfish. You can eat and cook exactly what you're in the mood for and no one else comes into the equation.

What you don't want is to be using too much brainpower, trying to work out what to cook for yourself or doing the complicated maths of scaling down a recipe you like the look of. Sadly, heating up a bought meal for one often starts to seem like the only option. Fear not, there are so many things you can do just for one in hardly any time at all, and they will taste far better than any ready-made meal. Cooking something for yourself that you really want to eat makes you feel good and certainly improves your mood if you are feeling stressed, tired or lonely.

These are some of my favourite recipes, using good healthy ingredients that are easy to get hold of if you don't already have food in. And don't worry, you won't have to buy in large quantities and then find you never use the rest up. Everything serves one nicely. If you like, they can even be scaled up to serve two or more, without the maths being too complicated.

If I'm feeling really hungry and am low on supplies, one of my reliable favourites is beans on toast — with a difference. I like to give my beans a Bloody Mary twist by adding a few drops of Tabasco, a spoon of horseradish sauce and a good shake of Worcestershire sauce to the pan with the beans. It's delicious and you somehow feel like you've done some cooking.

Greek Lamb Pitta Salad

This is amazingly easy to put together and just because you're cooking for one, doesn't mean you have to compromise on flavour and quality ingredients. If you can only buy lamb fillets or steaks in packs of two, then put one in the freezer ready to use another time when the mood takes you.

* **serves one**
  takes 10 to 15 minutes to make

Heat the olive oil in a frying pan. Season the lamb with salt and pepper and fry over a high heat for a few minutes until cooked through. Add the peas to the pan and toss around until they are heated through too.

Tip into a bowl and toss together with the feta, mint or coriander, olives and cucumber. Squeeze over the lemon juice and add a good glug of olive oil. Season again and spoon on to a plate.

Serve with a big spoonful of hummus, if using, and some toasted or grilled pitta or flat bread.

1 tablespoon olive oil

1 lamb fillet or leg steak, cut into strips

sea salt and freshly ground black pepper

a small handful of frozen peas, defrosted

100g feta cheese, crumbled

mint or coriander leaves, roughly chopped

a few black Greek olives

¼ cucumber, chopped

½ lemon

extra-virgin olive oil

hummus (optional)

pitta bread or flat bread

PS...*Strips of chicken or a fresh tuna steak can be used instead of the lamb.*

Honey-seared Salmon with Sesame Noodles

I like to make this when I'm in the mood for something light and nutritious — usually when I'm feeling healthy but starving hungry after a stint at the gym. This dish takes about ten minutes to prepare. What are you waiting for? Go!

* serves one
takes about 20 minutes to make

Cook the noodles according to the packet instructions and drain. Toss in a teaspoon of the sesame oil to prevent them sticking together.

Toss the salmon with the honey and soy sauce. Heat a non-stick frying pan or wok over a high heat. Add the sesame seeds, toast until they are lightly golden, and then remove from the pan. Add a teaspoon of sesame oil to the pan and, once hot, cook the salmon for about a minute each side or until golden (reserving any of the honey and soy left behind in the dish). Remove from the pan and keep warm.

Add the remaining teaspoon of sesame oil to the pan and quickly fry the noodles, spring onion and bean sprouts until the noodles are heated through. Add the spinach, sesame seeds and any remaining honey and soy mixture from the salmon. Toss until the spinach is starting to wilt.

Tip the noodles and spinach mixture into a serving bowl. Sit the honey-seared salmon on top and serve straight away.

1 strip of egg or rice noodles

3 teaspoons sesame oil

1 salmon fillet, skinned and sliced into 2cm thick strips

2 teaspoons runny honey

2 teaspoons soy sauce

1 teaspoon sesame seeds

3–4 spring onions, sliced

a handful of bean sprouts

2 large handfuls of spinach leaves

1 teaspoon sesame seeds

PS . . . *For a bit of a kick, add a pinch of chilli flakes to the honey and soy sauce.*

The salmon can be swapped for prawns or strips of chicken, pork or beef.

Frozen Pea and Mascarpone Soup

Perfect for a weekend lunch or a simple supper when you're short of supplies. Oh, by the way, this can be made in the time it takes to hand wash your favourite jumper!

* serves two
 takes 10 minutes to make

Heat the oil in a saucepan and sauté the onion for about 5 minutes until it's softened but not coloured. Add the stock and as soon as it is boiling, add the peas. Return to the boil and cook for 3 minutes. Stir in the mascarpone and the basil or mint and season with salt and pepper.

Blitz the soup in a food processor or blender or using a hand blender until smooth. Serve with some chunky bread.

1 tablespoon olive oil

1 small onion, chopped

400ml chicken or
 vegetable stock

275g frozen peas

4 tablespoons mascarpone cheese

2 tablespoons chopped basil
 or mint

sea salt and freshly ground
 black pepper

PS... *You can add chopped ham and a few more whole peas to the soup for a chunkier texture.*

For some accompaniments, try frying chopped streaky bacon or pancetta to scatter over the top. If you have any bread to hand, tear it into cubes and put on a baking sheet. Pound together 2 tablespoons of olive oil, a good pinch of salt and 1 tablespoon of basil or mint in a pestle and mortar. Pour over the bread, toss around and bake briefly in a hot oven to give instant herby croutons.

Fiery Roast Pepper Soup

This is a great one for a cold night when you are in the mood for something spicy to warm you up from top to toe. It's really effortless because all you do is throw the veggies in a roasting tray, roast in the oven, and then blend with some stock to create a thick and filling soup. Serve with some focaccia or crusty ciabatta to dunk in.

* **serves four to six**

**takes 1 hour to make
(most of which is roasting time)**

Preheat the oven to 200°C/fan 180°C/gas 6.

Place the peppers, carrots, chilli, garlic and tomatoes in a large roasting tray and toss them in the paprika and olive oil. Season with salt and pepper and roast in the oven for about 40 minutes until the vegetables are softened and beginning to char around the edges.

Cool slightly and place the vegetables in a blender with the stock (this may need to be done in two batches, depending on the size of your machine). Blitz to a chunky or smooth consistency, whichever you prefer, and transfer to a clean saucepan.

Heat the soup gently, then ladle it into bowls and add a dollop of crème fraîche and an extra sprinkle of paprika or twist of black pepper to serve.

4 red peppers,
  halved and deseeded

3 carrots, peeled and
  quartered lengthways

1 long red chilli, halved

2 cloves of garlic

500g ripe tomatoes, halved

2 teaspoons paprika

3 tablespoons olive oil

sea salt and freshly ground
  black pepper

800ml vegetable stock

crème fraîche

PS... *Crispy fried slices of chorizo or salami scattered over the top are a great addition to this soup.*

Prawn and Coconut Satay Broth

A delicious Thai-style stir-fry and broth in one, which uses two simple ingredients, peanut butter and coconut milk, to make a quick satay sauce. You can take the prawns out altogether and add extra vegetables, such as bean sprouts or thinly sliced peppers, for a vegetarian broth. Alternatively, cook strips of chicken or pork with the garlic for a meaty version. Serve in a deep bowl with chopsticks and a spoon.

* **serves two**
  takes about 10 minutes to make

Cook the noodles according to the packet instructions.

While they are cooking, heat the oil in a wok or large saucepan and briefly fry the garlic. Stir in the peanut butter and coconut milk to make a loose paste before adding the stock.

Bring to a simmer and add the prawns, spring onion, chilli flakes and soy sauce. Cook for 2 to 3 minutes until the prawns are heated through, and then add the cooked and drained noodles.

Return to a simmer and finally add a squeeze of lime juice and the fresh coriander. Serve straight away.

- 2 strips of medium egg noodles
- 1 tablespoon vegetable oil
- 1 clove of garlic, crushed
- 2 tablespoons smooth or crunchy peanut butter
- 200ml coconut milk
- 500ml chicken or vegetable stock
- 200g cooked king prawns, defrosted if frozen
- 1 bunch of spring onions, thinly sliced
- a pinch of dried chilli flakes
- 1 teaspoon soy sauce
- a squeeze of lime juice
- a large handful of coriander, roughly chopped

PS . . . *Use the rest of the can of coconut milk to make a tropical smoothie by blending with some banana, fresh or tinned lychees, pineapple and mango.*

In the mood for a drink? *Gewürztraminer is akin to spicy rose Turkish delight — it'll work brilliantly with this dish. For an alternative, the white Verdelho grape variety is simpler and stunning.*

Parmesan-crusted Chicken with Avocado Salad

The perfect recipe to impress a friend you've invited round for a quick bite to eat. The thin fillets of chicken stay remarkably juicy when coated in egg white and the sticky Parmesan crust is so yummy. All you need is a glass of chilled white wine and you will have a delicious, hassle-free dinner.

* serves two
takes about 20 minutes to make

First of all, make the salad by just lightly mixing everything together. Leave to one side while you prepare the chicken.

Slice each chicken breast in half to give you four thin, flat pieces. Mix the chilli powder into the Parmesan and place on a plate or in a shallow dish. Crack the egg white into a shallow dish and lightly whisk.

Dip the chicken into the egg, and then press into the Parmesan cheese, thoroughly coating the pieces on both sides.

Heat the olive oil in a frying pan over a high heat. Cook the chicken for 1 to 2 minutes each side until golden and crisp. Serve two pieces of the juicy Parmesan chicken each, with a lemon wedge to squeeze over and the avocado salad on the side.

for the salad

1 ripe avocado, sliced

½ red onion, thinly sliced

2 ripe, juicy tomatoes, cut into thin wedges, or a small punnet of cherry or baby plum tomatoes, halved

1 teaspoon balsamic vinegar

1 tablespoon olive oil

a small handful of shredded basil leaves

sea salt and freshly ground black pepper

for the chicken

2 chicken breasts

a pinch of chilli powder

50g Parmesan cheese, finely grated

1 large egg white

1 tablespoon olive oil

lemon wedges

PS . . . *The salad makes a great dish on its own with some feta, mozzarella or goat's cheese scattered over the top.*

In the mood for a drink? *Full-bodied Chardonnay works, and if you fancy a glass of red, check out Grenache.*

Tomato, Ricotta and Basil Tart

For a light lunch or speedy dinner, this looks really impressive and is great to serve when you're entertaining and short of time.

* **serves four to six**

   takes only 10 minutes to throw together and 25 minutes to cook

Preheat the oven to 200°C/fan 180°C/gas 6.

Place the pastry on to a lightly oiled baking tray and prick several times with a fork.

Mix together the ricotta, eggs, Parmesan, garlic, basil and seasoning and beat until smooth. Spread over the pastry base, leaving about a 2cm border.

Arrange the tomatoes on top of the ricotta, lining them up neatly or just randomly and pressing down gently. Season lightly and drizzle over a little olive oil.

Bake for 25 minutes until the filling has set and the pastry is golden. Serve with a nice green salad dressed with balsamic vinegar and olive oil or just as it is.

375g ready-rolled puff pastry

250g ricotta cheese

2 large eggs, lightly beaten

35g Parmesan cheese, grated

1 clove of garlic, crushed

a large bunch of basil leaves, finely shredded

sea salt and freshly ground black pepper

6 ripe tomatoes, halved

olive oil

PS...*Sliced black olives, anchovies or capers are very tasty scattered over the tart just before cooking.*

In the mood for a drink? *Sauvignon Blanc is zippy enough to cope with the acidity of the tomatoes without swamping the ricotta. For a bargain look at France's Loire region; for pungency, check out Marlborough Sauvignon Blancs from New Zealand.*

Corner Shop Curry

Just about everyone has a corner shop within walking distance. They're great in an emergency because they stock all sorts of useful ingredients. This curry is so lovely it's hard to believe it's made from such basic everyday ingredients. The vegetables I have suggested are just a guide, so if your corner shop doesn't have some of them, just change the selection to suit whatever you can find.

* serves four

takes about 50 minutes to make (most of which is cooking time)

Heat the oil in a saucepan and gently fry the onion until it has softened. Add the garlic, potato, carrot, pepper and curry powder. Cook for about 5 minutes until the vegetables are just starting to soften and become golden. Stir in the tomatoes, stock and lemon juice, bring to a simmer and cook for 30 minutes.

Stir in the chickpeas and continue to cook for a further 5 minutes for the chickpeas to heat through.

By now the vegetables should be tender and the sauce thick. Stir in the yoghurt or cream and season with salt. Serve with rice, naan bread or whatever you fancy.

2 tablespoons sunflower or vegetable oil

1 onion, chopped

2 cloves of garlic, crushed

2–3 potatoes, peeled and cut into chunks

2 carrots, cut into chunks

1 green or red pepper, deseeded and cut into chunks

3 tablespoons mild, medium or hot curry powder

400g tin of chopped tomatoes

200ml vegetable stock

juice of 1/2 lemon

400g tin of chickpeas, drained

4 tablespoons natural yoghurt or cream

sea salt

PS . . . *If your corner shop sells it, coconut milk or coconut cream can be used instead of the natural yoghurt or cream, while a small tin of drained pineapple chunks adds a delicious fruity flavour.*

The curry also benefits from a few fresh herbs, so if you have any coriander or parsley, stir it into the curry at the end.

In the mood for a drink? *Cold lager is a convenient and popular option; chilled Cava works beautifully; or you could bring out the heat with a deeply flavoured spicy red such as Shiraz.*

Ginger and Banana Trifles

Well, more of a trifle with a difference really.

* makes four
takes 10 minutes to make

Take four glasses or dishes and layer up the ginger cake with the banana, half the ginger, the ginger syrup, orange juice, Cointreau or Grand Marnier. Finish off by topping with a spoonful of cream, crème fraîche or Greek yoghurt. Sprinkle over the remaining ginger to serve.

4 thick slices of bought
  Jamaica ginger cake,
  cut into pieces

2 bananas, sliced

1 ball of stem ginger
  (from a jar), finely chopped

1 tablespoon ginger syrup
  from the jar of stem ginger

2 tablespoons orange juice,
  Cointreau or Grand Marnier

4 large spoonfuls of whipped
  cream, crème fraîche
  or Greek yoghurt

Orange Caramel Yoghurt

* serves two
takes 10 minutes to make

Using a sharp knife, cut off the skin and pith from the oranges and thinly slice. Place in the base of two dishes and spoon over the yoghurt.

Scatter over the sugar and leave for just a few minutes for the sugar to dissolve and create a caramel syrup. The longer you leave it, the more the caramel dissolves into the yoghurt.

2 large juicy oranges

250–350ml Greek yoghurt

2 tablespoons dark or light
  soft brown sugar or
  muscovado sugar

Emergency Zone
Storecupboard suppers

You're desperate for something to eat and you want it now. You look in the fridge and in your cupboard, but nothing jumps out at you (I don't mean literally). You're so hungry, even a trip to the supermarket is too long to wait.

Well, look around your kitchen again and you might be really surprised at just what you can throw together with simple, everyday ingredients. I have a few favourite recipes that I know I can turn to when I find myself in times of need, made just from ingredients I usually have in my cupboard and fridge.

Now, if you've looked long and hard and all you seem to have in there is a sad old jar of mustard (or at least that's what you think it is) and loads of out-of-date packets, tins and jars, then the next time you go shopping, stock up on some basics. That way you can turn to the recipes here when a real hunger emergency occurs and you'll know there is a solution in your cupboard.

Opposite is a list of what you'll need to be stocked up on for the following recipes.

in your cupboard

* a tin of whole or chopped tomatoes
* a tin of white beans, such as cannellini, butter beans or chickpeas
* sweetcorn
* dried herbs, such as a jar of mixed or individual jars of thyme, oregano and rosemary
* dried spices, such as turmeric, coriander, cumin, chilli powder and chilli flakes
* olive oil, both virgin and extra-virgin
* chilli oil
* sesame oil
* Tabasco sauce
* rice vinegar
* tomato ketchup
* dried egg noodles
* dried pasta
* sultanas and/or raisins
* cashew nuts, walnuts and peanuts
* jam
* baking powder
* plain flour
* caster sugar
* loaf of bread (keep some as backup in the freezer too)
* sea salt and black pepper

in the fridge

* large eggs
* milk
* cheese, such as Parmesan, Cheddar and a blue cheese if you are a fan
* butter
* natural yoghurt
* oyster sauce
* mayonnaise
* soy sauce
* baking potatoes

* garlic
* onions (red and white)
* spring onions
* cucumber
* tomatoes
* apples
* lemons and limes
* parsley, basil, coriander and mint (try and keep a pot of each on the go if you can't keep them fresh in the fridge)

not essential, but extremely useful

* a tin or jar of anchovies
* a tin of tuna
* olives
* pickled chillies
* gherkins
* marinated peppers
* marinated artichokes
* sundried tomatoes
* sweet chilli sauce
* vanilla extract
* brioche (it has a longer shelf life than other fresh breads)
* tortilla wraps (not essential, but great as again they have a longer shelf life than most breads)
* breadsticks
* baked beans (they're not in any of the recipes, but no cupboard is complete without a tin of beans)
* avocado
* watercress
* bacon
* smoked salmon
* ham or a packet of cured meat, such as chorizo, salami or Parma ham
* prawns (in the freezer)
* crème fraîche, sour cream or double cream
* ice cream

Tomato Pizza Toast

*** serves one or two
takes 10 to 15 minutes to make**

Heat up the tomatoes with a sprinkle of the dried herbs and a good pinch of sea salt and freshly ground black pepper. Bring to the boil to reduce the quantity of tomato juice a bit.

Toast the bread and drizzle with olive oil. Once the tomatoes have thickened, spoon on to the toasted bread and grate over some Parmesan or Cheddar cheese. Eat straight away or grill to completely melt the cheese.

400g tin of whole or chopped tomatoes

a sprinkle of dried herbs (mixed, oregano, thyme or rosemary)

sea salt and freshly ground black pepper

bread (anything will do, but thickly sliced is best)

olive oil

Parmesan or Cheddar cheese

PS . . . Feel free to add any other pizza toppings you can find, such as anchovies, tuna, olives, ham, marinated peppers or artichokes and sundried tomatoes.

Nutty Noodles

*** serves one
takes 10 minutes to make**

Cook the egg noodles according to the packet instructions and drain.

Toss the noodles in a little chilli oil and the oyster sauce. Add the spring onion, a squeeze of lime juice or a splash of rice vinegar and the coriander.

Scatter over the cashew nuts or peanuts and serve.

a strip of thin or medium egg noodles

chilli oil

1 tablespoon oyster sauce

2 spring onions, shredded

a squeeze of lime juice or a splash of rice vinegar

a small handful of chopped coriander (if you have some)

chopped cashew nuts or peanuts, to serve

Spicy Cheese and Tomato on Toast

This is my favourite way of making cheese on toast.

* **serves two to four**
  takes about 10 minutes to make

Preheat the grill.

Toast the bread in a toaster or under the grill.

Mix together the remaining ingredients and spread on to the toast, completely covering it. Cook under the grill until the cheese is golden and bubbling. Serve straight away.

4 slices of bread

½ small red onion, finely chopped

200g grated mature Cheddar cheese

2 tomatoes, finely chopped

½ teaspoon mild chilli powder or a few drops of Tabasco sauce

a small handful of parsley, coriander or basil leaves, roughly chopped (optional)

1 heaped tablespoon mayonnaise or tomato ketchup

Blue Cheese, Walnut and Apple on Toast

Bit of a posh version of cheese on toast. Stilton, Danish Blue, Cashel Blue or any crumbly blue cheese can be used for this.

* **serves two to four**
  takes 10 to 15 minutes to make

Preheat the grill. Toast the bread in a toaster or under the grill.

Place the apple and onion in a sieve and squeeze away all of the excess liquid by pressing down with the back of a spoon. Transfer to a bowl and mix with the cheese and walnuts. Season with the pepper and some salt if the cheese isn't too salty.

Divide the mixture among the toasts so it completely covers them, place on a baking sheet and grill until the cheese is bubbling.

Serve straight away, with watercress if you have some.

4 slices of bread

1 eating apple with the skin left on, grated

½ red onion, grated

200g crumbled blue cheese, whatever you fancy

75g walnut pieces

sea salt (if needed) and freshly ground black pepper

Sweetcorn and Chilli Pancakes

Perfect for when you crave something savoury and substantial for breakfast right the way through to a midnight snack. It's amazing what you can throw together when you really look around your kitchen.

* **makes about ten**
  takes about 15 minutes to make

Beat together the flour, baking powder, chilli powder, eggs and milk until you have a smooth batter. Stir in the sweetcorn, onion, coriander or parsley and some seasoning.

Heat a little olive oil in a non-stick frying pan or pancake pan. Drop 2 tablespoons of batter per fritter into the pan and cook as many as will fit comfortably for a couple of minutes until the bases are golden. Carefully turn over and cook for a further 2 minutes, again until the bases are golden.

Keep warm while you continue with the remaining batter, adding more oil to the pan as you go.

200g plain flour

2 teaspoons baking powder

1/2 teaspoon mild chilli powder

3 eggs, beaten

100ml milk

300g tin of sweetcorn, drained

4–6 spring onions, chopped,
  or 1/2 red onion,
    finely chopped

1 tablespoon chopped
  coriander or parsley

sea salt and freshly ground
  black pepper

olive oil

PS...*All sorts of things can be served with the pancakes, such as:*
* *Crispy fried bacon.*
* *Roasted peppers.*
* *Smoked salmon.*
* *Fried chorizo or salami.*
* *Cooked prawns.*
* *Grilled halloumi cheese.*
* *Sliced avocado or guacamole.*
* *Pickled chillies and gherkins.*
* *Sour cream or crème fraîche.*
* *Sweet chilli dipping sauce.*
* *Tomato ketchup.*

Hot Jam Sandwich

These would convert Paddington Bear from marmalade to jam. Quick, delicious and different. A hot jam sandwich, I hear you say? Try them now!

＊ makes one
takes about 10 minutes to make

Lightly beat together the egg, caster sugar and vanilla extract in a shallow dish.

Sandwich the bread and jam together, pressing firmly so it sticks. Melt the butter in a large frying pan over a low-medium heat.

Soak the sandwich in the egg mixture until all of the egg has been absorbed. Fry in the butter for 1 to 2 minutes each side until golden brown.

Slice the sandwich in half or into fingers, sprinkle with the caster sugar and enjoy straight away with a scoop of ice cream, crème fraîche, yoghurt, cream or just as it is.

1 large egg

2 teaspoons caster sugar,
plus extra to sprinkle

a few drops of vanilla extract
(optional)

2 slices of brioche or white bread

1–2 tablespoons of your favourite
jam (black cherry is my
favourite)

a small knob of unsalted butter

Pasta Pronto
You can always rely on a bag of pasta

It's amazing how many types of pastas you can buy now. I really think it's the king of convenience food – I love it. Virtually anything goes, so a meal can be as simple as tossing cooked pasta in butter, black pepper and grated Parmesan or it can be something much more imaginative, yet still quick to prepare. If you're in the mood for being lazy and fancy some pasta, but the creative part of your brain has gone on a break, then have a look through my favourite sauces and flavours for some inspiration.

I tend to use dried pasta, mainly because there is always some in the cupboard. However, I also find it more versatile and less likely to become as stodgy as some of the fresh ones can, but it is entirely up to you, use whatever you prefer.

Spaghetti with Garlic and Chilli

So simple, but exceptionally tasty.

* **serves two**
  takes about 15 minutes to make

Cook the spaghetti until al dente.

While the pasta is cooking, heat the olive oil in a saucepan and gently fry the garlic and red chilli.

Drain the pasta, add to the sauce and toss until combined. Rocket or basil leaves can also be added here if you like. Season with sea salt and serve with Parmesan cheese sprinkled over the top.

PS . . . Tart this up by adding some white crabmeat to the pasta or cooking some raw tiger prawns with the garlic and chilli. If you do add seafood, then you may prefer not to use the Parmesan.

200–300g spaghetti, linguine or spaghettini

2–3 tablespoons extra-virgin olive oil

2 cloves of garlic, thinly sliced or chopped

1 red chilli, thinly sliced (leave some seeds in for an extra-spicy flavour)

rocket or basil leaves (optional)

sea salt

Parmesan cheese

Pesto Pasta Special

A great recipe using simple, everyday ingredients.

* **serves as many as you like**
  takes about 15 minutes to make

Cook the pasta until al dente and drain.

Toss the pasta with the balsamic vinegar, some green or red pesto sauce and olive oil, the tomato and red onion. Chuck in a few olives.

Serve warm with a good sprinkling of sea salt, black pepper and Parmesan cheese.

as much pasta as you fancy (it really depends on how hungry you are or how many people you are cooking for)

a splash of balsamic vinegar

green or red pesto sauce

olive oil

1 ripe tomato, chopped

1 red onion, finely chopped

a few olives (if you have them)

sea salt and freshly ground black pepper

Parmesan cheese

Chorizo, Tomato, Rocket and Black Olive Penne

* **serves two**
  takes about 15 minutes to make

Cook the penne until al dente.

While the pasta is cooking, heat a drop of olive oil in a frying pan and fry the chorizo until crisp. Add the tomatoes and balsamic vinegar. Cook briefly until the tomatoes are starting to break down.

Drain the pasta, tip in the sauce and toss together with the rocket leaves and tapenade. Season with black pepper and divide between two bowls.

200–300g penne
olive oil
125g chorizo, sliced
250g cherry or baby plum tomatoes, halved
2 teaspoons balsamic vinegar
a bag (about 50g) of rocket
2–3 tablespoons tapenade
freshly ground black pepper

Zesty Olive, Parmesan and Basil Penne

Just because this uses only a few ingredients, doesn't mean it's short of flavour. Use the best olives you can and it will really make a difference.

* **serves two**
  takes about 15 minutes to make

Cook the pasta until al dente and drain, reserving about 2 tablespoons of the cooking liquid.

Toss the cooked pasta and cooking liquid with the olives, lemon zest and juice, the chopped basil and Parmesan cheese.

Add the olive oil and season well with sea salt and black pepper. Serve warm or cold.

200–300g penne
a handful of black or green olives (fat juicy ones in oil are best), halved
finely grated zest and juice of ½ lemon
a large handful of chopped basil
50g Parmesan cheese, grated
a glug of extra-virgin olive oil
sea salt and freshly ground black pepper

Courgette, Lemon and Crab Linguine

Use fresh crabmeat if you can get some; if not, then tinned will do. This has an extravagant taste and is great to serve to friends if you don't want to spend long in the kitchen, but still want to impress.

* **serves four**
takes about 15 minutes to make

Cook the linguine until al dente.

Meanwhile, heat 3 tablespoons of olive oil in a frying pan and gently sauté the courgette, red onion and red chilli until soft and slightly golden.

Add the lemon zest, capers and white crabmeat. Season with sea salt and black pepper.

Drain the linguine and toss with the sauce. Add some extra olive oil and the lemon juice to create a dressing and serve straight away.

400–500g linguine
olive oil
2 large courgettes, thinly sliced
1 large red onion, thinly sliced
1 red chilli, deseeded and
  thinly sliced
grated zest and juice of
  1 lemon
2 tablespoons capers, rinsed
200–300g white crabmeat
sea salt and freshly ground
  black pepper

Smoked Salmon and Leek Tagliatelle

Combining white wine and mascarpone cheese creates a lovely light, yet rich base for this exceptionally tasty sauce.

* **serves two**
takes about 15 minutes to make

Cook the tagliatelle until al dente.

While the pasta is cooking, sauté the leeks in some olive oil. Stir in the white wine, the dried chilli flakes or thyme and the mascarpone cheese. Heat until the mascarpone has melted.

Stir in the smoked salmon. Drain the pasta and toss with the sauce.

200–300g tagliatelle
2 medium leeks, sliced
olive oil
a glass of white wine
a pinch of dried chilli flakes
  or fresh or dried thyme
200g mascarpone cheese
4 slices of smoked salmon, cut
  into strips

A Simple Tomato Sauce

This is such a versatile sauce. Not only is it great for tossing into pasta just as it is, but it can also be added to sautéed chicken, cooked prawns or used as a sauce to serve with grilled or barbecued fish.

* serves four
  takes about 30 minutes to make

Place the tomatoes in a saucepan with the dried chilli flakes, crushed garlic, olive oil, balsamic vinegar, caster sugar and a good pinch of sea salt and black pepper. Bring to a simmer and cook over a low heat for 20 to 30 minutes until the sauce is rich and thick.

If you want a creamy sauce, stir in the cream cheese or mascarpone.

2 x 400g tins of tomatoes

1–2 teaspoons dried chilli flakes

2 cloves of garlic, crushed

3 tablespoons olive oil

1 teaspoon balsamic vinegar

1 teaspoon caster sugar

sea salt and freshly ground black pepper

100g cream cheese or mascarpone (optional)

Flaked Tuna and Salsa Verde Pasta Salad

A lovely pasta salad that can also be made with cooked new potatoes instead of pasta.

* serves two
  takes about 15 minutes to make

Cook the penne until al dente.

Meanwhile, blitz together the parsley and basil leaves, capers, garlic, Dijon mustard, anchovy fillets, olive oil and the lemon zest and juice in a food processor or blender until it forms a rough paste.

Drain the pasta, refresh under the cold tap and toss in a little olive oil to prevent it from sticking. Toss the sauce with the cooked pasta and finally flake in the tuna.

200–300g penne or another short pasta shape

a handful of parsley and basil leaves

1 tablespoon capers, rinsed

1 clove of garlic

1 teaspoon Dijon mustard

2 anchovy fillets

2 tablespoons fruity extra-virgin olive oil

zest and juice of ½ lemon

200g tinned tuna in olive oil

In the Mood for Being
Extravagant

There are times when I really fancy pushing the boat out, going to town and being totally glam. Whether it's having a girly get-together, a full-on dinner party, a house packed with friends or just some tasty nibbles to have with drinks, I love that mood of being extravagant. It's a chance to really show off, be lavish and treat everyone, and yourself, to exceptional food and drink. The sort of food that is a step above your everyday usuals. Serving something extravagant will not only make your guests feel special, it will also make you feel fantastic when you're showered with compliments and praise.

Usually, you'll find that you're in the mood for being extravagant when there's a special occasion such as a birthday, house warming, a farewell or maybe a celebration such as finishing writing this book! But there are plenty of other times when there doesn't need to be a reason. Just having people round who you want to spend time with, tucking into some stylish yet simple food and drinks, is brilliant.

What I must point out, though, is that being extravagant doesn't equal stress — stress is not allowed! It shouldn't be about getting in a flap or panic. More often than not, the way you present food on a plate makes the world of difference, no matter how simple it is to prepare. Also, you'll find that as long as you buy good-quality ingredients, their flavours will speak for themselves, making it far easier to keep the preparation simple.

Why make hard work of things when you're in the mood for being extravagant? Just bear in mind that it should be about doing everything 'simply but exquisitely'.

Time for Tea
Treats for an afternoon get-together

When I'm in the mood for an extravagant afternoon tea, I have this romantic image in my head as to how I would like it — tiered cake stands, floral plates, beautiful china cups, silverware and pretty napkins, triangular sandwiches, cream cakes, pastries, iced tea or glasses of pink bubbly — I think you get the picture. I see it as an opportunity to feel like I have gone back in time to the grounds of an old country house, stopping for afternoon tea in between games of croquet or a spot of tennis on the lawn.

Traditionally, a formal afternoon tea is served in three stages. First of all, a pot of tea is brought out, though I think it is also nice to serve a jug of iced tea if the weather's hot. Secondly, it is customary to have a glass of champagne — fabulous! Finally, the food makes a grand appearance on a triple cake stand, comprising dainty sandwiches, scones and home-made miniature cakes and pastries. A slice of cake is optional — just in case you're still hungry.

Afternoon tea is a wonderfully sophisticated alternative to lunch or dinner, especially if you're in the mood for a good gossip with your closest friends. You can have a relaxing catch up without missing out on vital information going to and from the kitchen. All the preparation is done prior to your friends arriving, so there's no stress involved.

So, go full speed ahead on elegance and serve some delightful treats for a wonderful couple of hours. Even though we all lead busy lives, it's well worth making time for a good old-fashioned afternoon tea get together once in a while. I just wish we had time for afternoon tea every day.

Sandwiches

It wouldn't be a proper afternoon tea without sandwiches. Some of the classics such as cucumber and cream cheese, ham and mustard and smoked salmon are great, but to make a real impression these two are delightful. Don't forget to eat them nicely and hold your little finger out.

Chicken, Cress and Poppy Seed Tea Sandwiches

* **makes twenty small sandwiches**
   takes about 15 minutes to make

Mix together all but 1½ tablespoons of the mayonnaise with the mustard and chicken. Season with salt and pepper and spread over five slices of the bread. Top with the cress and the remaining slices of bread, pressing down lightly. Remove the crusts and cut into triangular quarters.

Place the poppy seeds on a plate. Sparingly spread the extra mayonnaise on to just one edge of the sandwich quarters. Dip into the seeds and place on a clean plate.

100g mayonnaise

2 teaspoons Dijon mustard

250g cooked chicken breast, shredded

sea salt and freshly ground black pepper

10 medium slices of white bread

2 tubs of salad or mustard cress

2 tablespoons poppy seeds

Smoked Salmon and Radish Fingers with Tarragon Butter

* **makes fifteen small sandwiches**
   takes about 15 minutes to make

Mix together the butter, tarragon and lemon juice. Season with a little salt and pepper, and then spread on all the bread slices.

Place the smoked salmon and radish on five slices of the bread and top with the remaining slices. Trim away the crusts and cut each one into three fingers. Arrange on a nice plate to serve.

75g softened butter

2 tablespoons chopped tarragon

a good squeeze of lemon juice

sea salt and freshly ground black pepper

10 thin slices of brown bread

5–10 slices of smoked salmon

6–8 radishes, very thinly sliced

Mini Cream Slices

These exceptionally dainty puff pastry squares, sandwiched together with vanilla cream and topped with fruit, are perfect for afternoon tea. If you are going all out and serving these in the traditional way, they should be arranged on the top tier of a three-tiered cake stand, with scones in the middle (or try the lemon cheesecake 'muffins' on page 201 as a luxurious alternative) and dainty sandwiches (see page 195) on the bottom.

* **makes twenty to twenty-four**
  takes 20 to 25 minutes to make

Heat the oven to 200°C/fan 180°C/gas 6.

Cut the pastry into 4cm squares. Brush the tops with the egg wash and sprinkle with 1 tablespoon of the sugar. Sit on a baking sheet and bake for 7 to 8 minutes until they are golden and puffed up. Remove from the oven and leave to cool.

Whisk the cream with the remaining 2 tablespoons of the sugar and the vanilla extract until fairly firm peaks form.

Split the pastry squares in half (this should be really easy, with the top half just popping off). Place a spoonful of cream inside each base and sit the other half of the pastry on top.

Add a small spoonful of cream on top of each cream sandwich, decorate with fruit and dust with icing sugar to serve.

½ pack (about 190g)
  ready-rolled puff pastry
1 egg yolk, beaten with
  1 teaspoon milk
3 tablespoons caster sugar
250ml double cream
½ teaspoon vanilla extract
fruit, such as strawberries,
  raspberries, peaches,
    nectarines, bananas, kiwis,
    mangoes or blueberries,
    to decorate
icing sugar

Lemon Cheesecake 'Muffins'

These light and tangy individual cheesecakes are made in muffin cases and are a very impressive treat to offer for afternoon tea. More importantly, they're a doddle to make. Limes or oranges can be used in place of the lemons, not only giving you a new flavour but also making different pastel-coloured cheesecakes.

* **makes eight**

**takes about 20 minutes to make,
plus 3 hours setting time**

Line a muffin tin with eight large paper muffin cases.

Mix together the butter, crushed biscuits and ginger, and then press firmly into the base of the cases (this is easily done by using the base of a small glass). Keep in the fridge while you make the filling.

To make the filling, top the lemon juice up with water to give you 100ml of liquid. Place in a small pan and heat until it's hot but not quite boiling. Sprinkle over the gelatine and stir briskly until it has dissolved. Leave to cool to room temperature.

Beat the cream cheese, crème fraîche, honey and lemon zest until smooth, and then stir in the cooled lemon juice.

Whip the egg whites until they form soft peaks and fold into the lemony cream cheese mixture. Spoon the mixture on to the chilled bases, smoothing the tops with the back of a teaspoon.

Chill in the fridge for about 3 hours until set. Decorate with sugared flowers or frosted rose petals just before serving.

100g butter, melted

**150g digestive biscuits,
finely crushed**

**1 ball of stem ginger
(from a jar), finely chopped**

**finely grated zest and juice
of 2 lemons**

1 sachet of powdered gelatine

225g cream cheese

150ml crème fraîche

100ml runny honey

2 large egg whites

**sugared flowers or frosted rose
petals (see PS...), to decorate**

PS... If you prefer to use leaf gelatine, then soak four leaves in cold water for a few minutes until they soften. Squeeze out the excess water and stir into the hot lemon juice until they dissolve. Continue with the rest of the recipe as above.

To frost rose petals, dip individual petals into a lightly whisked egg white, allowing the excess to drip off, and then gently coat in caster sugar. Leave to dry on a plate before using to decorate the cheesecakes. Any leftovers can be stored in an airtight container.

When Only Bubbly Will Do

If you're partial to a drop of bubbly, whether it's champagne or sparkling wine, then you'll love these fruity cocktails.

St Clement's Champagne

* **makes one**

Mix together the Cointreau and limoncello in a Champagne flute and top up with Champagne.

Hold the orange zest, peeled-side up, between your thumb and forefinger about 10cm above the glass. Gently warm the zest with a lighter flame. Pinch the peel so that the orange oil falls through the flame into the drink. It will flash and spit a little, but adds a wonderfully intense orange flavour to the cocktail. Finish off by running the zest around the rim of the glass.

15ml (1 tablespoon) Cointreau

15ml (1 tablespoon) limoncello (Italian lemon liqueur)

chilled Champagne or sparkling wine, to top up

a 2cm strip of thinly peeled orange zest

Elderflower Champagne

* **makes six to eight glasses**

Divide up the elderflower cordial and lime juice among six to eight Champagne flutes. Top up with the chilled Champagne, mixing with a cocktail stirrer or straw as you pour.

4 tablespoons elderflower cordial

4 tablespoons freshly squeezed lime juice (about 2 limes)

1 bottle of chilled Champagne or sparkling wine

Thai-spiced Crab on Pineapple

A dainty canapé that is fresh, fruity and a little bit spicy. Arrange the bite-sized pieces of crab-topped pineapple neatly on to a flat plate and hand round with some little napkins for any sticky fingers.

* **makes about sixteen to eighteen**
  takes about 15 minutes to make

Slice the top, base and skin from the pineapple and cut the flesh into small bite-sized pieces, removing the core first if it seems tough.

Mix together the crab, chilli, sesame oil, lemon grass, spring onion, fish sauce, lime juice and coriander in a bowl. Spoon the mixture on top of the pineapple pieces, finish with a sprinkling of chopped peanuts and arrange on a serving plate.

½ **small pineapple**

75g **white crabmeat, fresh, frozen or tinned**

1–2 **teaspoons finely chopped red chilli**

½ **teaspoon sesame oil**

1 **teaspoon finely chopped lemon grass**

1 **spring onion, finely chopped**

½ **teaspoon fish sauce**

a squeeze of lime juice

1 **tablespoon chopped coriander**

1 **tablespoon finely chopped roasted peanuts**

PS . . . *Tinned tuna can be used instead of crab. If you can't get a fresh pineapple, again tinned will be fine (not quite as tasty, but a good alternative for emergencies).*

Peanut Prawns on Cucumber

Cucumber makes a great base for a canapé: refreshing, not too filling and easy to pick up with one hand.

*** makes twenty
takes about 15 minutes to make**

Slice the cucumber into twenty discs, each about 5mm thick.

Mix together the cream cheese, chilli sauce, spring onion, lemon juice and two-thirds of the peanuts. Spoon the mixture on top of the cucumber discs (to make them look neater, scoop the mixture between two teaspoons to give a nice shape).

Sit a prawn on top of each cucumber disc. Sprinkle over the remaining chopped peanuts and arrange on a serving plate.

½ **cucumber**

100g cream cheese

**2 teaspoons sweet
chilli dipping sauce**

2 spring onions, finely chopped

a squeeze of lemon juice

**75g dry roasted peanuts,
finely chopped**

**20 cooked and peeled
king prawns**

Sweet 'n' Spicy Nuts

These are the 'must-have' nibble for your cocktail party. They beat dry-roasted peanuts any day.

* takes 15 minutes to make

Preheat the oven to 200°C/fan 180°C/gas 6.

In a large bowl, lightly whisk the egg white until it is frothy. Add the nuts, spices, sugar, salt and a good twist of pepper and stir until the nuts are evenly coated.

Spread out the nuts in a single layer on a lightly oiled non-stick baking sheet. Roast in the oven for 8 to 10 minutes until the mixture has dried.

Allow the sweet and spicy nuts to cool for a few minutes. Break up any that have stuck together before serving with your fave cocktail.

1 egg white

**400g mixed nuts,
such as whole brazils, pecans,
blanched almonds
and hazelnuts**

¼ **teaspoon ground allspice**

¼ **teaspoon ground cinnamon**

½ **teaspoon cayenne pepper**

3 tablespoons demerara sugar

½ **teaspoon sea salt**

freshly ground black pepper

Cherry Tomatoes with Creamy Goat's Cheese and Caviar

These really will make you look like a professional. They're very stylish and yet so easy to put together. They can also be made well ahead of time and kept in the fridge until needed, allowing you plenty of time to decide what to wear.

*** makes thirty
takes about ½ hour to make**

Cut the base off each of the cherry tomatoes and scoop out the seeds. Turn them upside down and sit on kitchen paper to absorb any tomato juices from inside.

In a bowl, mix together the goat's cheese, cream and chopped chives and season with salt and pepper. This can now be spooned or piped (piping looks more stylish) into the hollowed-out tomatoes.

Cut the chives for the garnish into 1cm lengths. Top each tomato with a little caviar and a couple of pieces of chive.

These cute little tomatoes can be kept in the fridge until you are ready to serve them on a large platter.

30 cherry tomatoes
(try to get big ones rather than tiny ones)

150g soft goat's cheese

2 tablespoons single or whipping cream

1 tablespoon chopped chives

sea salt and freshly ground black pepper

chives, to garnish

2 tablespoons caviar

PS . . . *Soft goat's cheese has a really mild flavour, however if you're not a goat's cheese fan, you can use cream cheese. Black olive tapenade, sliced black olives or just chopped chives can be used as an alternative to the caviar.*

Mini Chorizo Toad-in-the-holes

One for the boys or for those of you who prefer a more substantial nibble.

* makes eighteen
  takes about 25 minutes to make

Preheat the oven to 200°C/fan 180°C/gas 6.

Place the chorizos into the cups of two mini muffin tins (you may have to make these in two batches if you don't have enough tins). Add a few drops of oil to each one and place in the oven for about 5 minutes so they heat through and the tin is lovely and hot.

Meanwhile, whisk together the flour, salt, egg, milk, Parmesan and thyme leaves until smooth.

Place a sunblush or sundried tomato in each of the muffin cups with the chorizo and fill with the batter. Put straight back into the oven.

Cook for 10 to 12 minutes until risen and golden. Serve straight away with a sprig of thyme on top of each one. If you are making these in advance, remove from the tins and reheat in the oven for 5 minutes when needed.

PS... *For any vegetarians, make as above but without the chorizo.*

18 small cocktail chorizo sausages
olive oil
50g plain flour
a pinch of sea salt
1 large egg
75ml milk
15g Parmesan cheese, grated
1 teaspoon thyme leaves
18 small sunblush
  or juicy sundried tomatoes
small sprigs of thyme, to garnish

Cheese (without Pineapple) on Sticks

Cheese and pineapple on sticks — what a classic, but not very original or sophisticated. So, to create more of a talking point, give some of these tasty variations a go.

Beetroot and Feta with Pesto

Cut pieces of baby beetroot in wedges and thread on to cocktail sticks with cubes of feta cheese. Just before serving, spoon over a little pesto that has been mixed with some olive oil to make a loose dressing.

Fig and Creamy Blue Cheese

Cut fresh figs into quarters and thread them on to cocktail sticks with a piece of a creamy blue cheese such as Gorgonzola or Dolcelatte. Serve at room temperature to enjoy the cheese at its best, adding a drizzle of olive oil and a twist of black pepper just before serving.

Melon, Parma Ham, Ricotta and Ginger

Very thinly slice a ball of stem ginger and thread individual slices on to cocktail sticks or skewers with cubes of ripe melon. Spoon a little ricotta cheese on to a slice of Parma ham, roll it up and slide on top of the melon and ginger. Mix two parts of the syrup from the jar of stem ginger with three parts olive oil and a good twist of black pepper. Just before serving, drizzle this dressing over the cocktail sticks.

Manchego, Quince and Caperberry

Cut a piece of Manchego cheese into bite-sized wedges and thread on to cocktail sticks or skewers with a slice of quince jelly and a large caperberry. Add a good twist of pepper.

Show Off
Stylish dinner party menus

So, you want to have a fabulous dinner party and really show off with the most amazing food, fine wines, your best crockery, cutlery, glasses, you name it, you want to do it. You can have the experience of a fancy restaurant in the relaxed surroundings of your own home with the real bonus that you create the mood by the way you arrange things. Maybe you want to be contemporary and keep the table decoration looking stylish and minimal, or perhaps a warm romantic feel with lots of candles and colour.

I love doing this. It's a chance to really shine and be given loads of compliments and praise. Well, come on, who doesn't like to be the centre of attention sometimes?

I've put together two wonderfully straightforward menus, each one to serve six people. They both require a little preparation ahead of time, but that will ensure a stress-free evening, leaving you to enjoy yourself as much as your guests.

Feel free to swap and change the menus around if you like. Just pick out whichever recipes take your fancy. After dessert, serve cheese and biscuits, then coffee and liqueurs (the choc 'n' nut liqueur on page 62 is perfect for this). If you fancy serving some petits fours with coffee, then why not make the chocolate, cherry and walnut brownies on page 65 and cut into mini squares, serving just one or two each.

Roast Sea Bass with White Wine Potatoes and Vine Tomatoes

The last thing you want when you're entertaining is a load of pots and pans at the end of a lovely meal, so this is perfect because it uses just one baking tray. Sea bass is one of my favourite fish and because it has such a delicate flavour, I think it's best to stick to simple flavours to go with it and not mess around trying to be too fancy.

*** serves six
takes about 40 minutes to make**

Preheat the oven to 200°C/fan 180°C/gas 6.

Cut the potatoes into 5mm thick slices. Place in a roasting tray with the red pepper and red onion, toss in 2 tablespoons olive oil and add a good pinch of salt. Roast for 15 minutes, turning a couple of times throughout.

Turn the potatoes in the tray again, add the white wine and return to the oven for 10 minutes.

Check the potatoes are almost cooked through. If not, return to the oven for 5 more minutes or so (adding a splash more wine if it has almost evaporated).

Place the sea bass on top of the potatoes with a sprig of rosemary under each one. Season with salt and pepper and sit the tomatoes on top of the fish. Drizzle with a little olive oil and return to the oven for 8–10 minutes until the fish looks cooked through and the tomatoes are beginning to split.

Remove the tray from the oven and divide the fish and vegetables among six warmed plates.

750g Charlotte potatoes
1 red pepper, deseeded
  and thinly sliced
1 large red onion, sliced
olive oil
sea salt and freshly
  ground black pepper
500ml white wine
6 sea bass fillets, skin on
6 sprigs of rosemary
6 branches of cherry vine
  tomatoes (with about
    6 tomatoes per vine)

PS . . . *If you fancy an accompanying salad, you could serve the dish with a peppery rocket and watercress salad.*

Marshmallow Meringues with Mango, Passion Fruit and Raspberries

I don't know about you, but I like meringues to have a crisp outside and a soft, fluffy marshmallow centre, which is exactly what these will give you. I am serving them as individual pavlovas, flavoured with mango and passion fruit cream and raspberries.

✳ serves six

**takes about 20 minutes to make,
plus 45 minutes to cook the meringues**

Preheat the oven to 140°C/fan 120°C/gas 1.

To make the meringues, whisk the egg whites until they form soft peaks. Add the caster sugar and continue to whisk for a couple of minutes.

Add the icing sugar, cornflour, lemon juice and vanilla extract. Whisk until you have a firm, glossy and super creamy consistency, a bit like shaving foam. This will take a good few minutes.

Place a piece of parchment paper on a baking sheet and lightly brush with a little of the sunflower or vegetable oil. Dollop and slightly swirl six large spoonfuls of the meringue on to the baking paper, leaving a space between each for them to spread slightly.

Bake for 45 minutes until the outsides are crispy but not coloured. Turn off the oven and leave to cool with the door slightly open. When the meringues have cooled, carefully peel away from the paper.

Place the mango in a blender and blitz until you have a smooth purée. If it doesn't taste very sweet, add a little sugar. Lightly whisk the cream until it literally just starts to form soft peaks. Swirl in the passion fruit seeds and the mango purée.

Sit the meringues on plates or dishes. Spoon the fruity cream on top and scatter over the raspberries. Then for the best part — crack into your meringue to reveal its soft centre. Oh, how impressed your friends will be.

for the meringues

4 large egg whites
100g caster sugar
125g icing sugar, sieved
1 teaspoon cornflour
1 teaspoon lemon juice
½ teaspoon vanilla extract
sunflower or vegetable oil

for the topping

2 small or 1 large ripe mango,
    peeled and roughly chopped
250ml double cream
3 passion fruit
200g raspberries

Warm Fig, Port and Blue Cheese Salad with a Pink Shallot and Walnut Dressing

You can prepare a lot of this recipe ahead of time so you won't miss out on any pre-dinner fun.

* serves six (as a starter)
takes 25 to 30 minutes to make

Preheat the oven to 200°C/fan 180°C/gas 6.

Start off by placing the shallots in a small dish and pouring over the red wine vinegar. Leave them to soak for about 10 minutes, stirring occasionally. This takes the rawness out of the shallots and also gives a nice flavour to the vinegar, which is going to be used for the dressing. Once the shallots have softened, remove them from the vinegar and keep to one side.

To make the dressing, place the shallot-flavoured red wine vinegar in a screw-top jar and add the walnut oil, olive oil, mustard, honey and seasoning. Put on the lid and shake well to give you a creamy dressing.

To prepare the figs, cut each one in half through its stalk, leaving the stalk attached. Place cut-side up in a small roasting tray and gently press down to open the fig up. Spoon a little port over each half.

Roast the figs for 3 to 5 minutes until tender but still holding their shape. Scatter the cheese and a twist of pepper over the top of each one and return to the oven for just 1 minute for the cheese to melt.

Sit a handful of salad leaves in the middle of six small or medium-sized plates and arrange the figs around the outside, spooning over any port juices from the roasting tray. Scatter the shallots and walnuts around the plate and over the leaves and finally drizzle over the dressing to serve.

for the dressing

4 shallots, cut into fairly thin rings

2 tablespoons red wine vinegar

4 tablespoons walnut oil

4 tablespoons extra-virgin olive oil

2 teaspoons Dijon mustard

2 teaspoons runny honey

sea salt and freshly ground black pepper

for the salad

9–12 ripe figs (depending on their size)

5–6 tablespoons port

100g Gorgonzola, Dolcelatte or Stilton cheese

freshly ground black pepper

6 small handfuls of watercress or rocket leaves

a handful of walnut pieces

PS . . . *If you can't get hold of any figs, you can substitute slices of pear. Use half a peeled, cored and sliced pear per person. Place in foil and fold up the edges to form a boat. Add the port and bake for 5 minutes to warm through. Continue as above, scattering over the cheese and returning to the oven for 1 minute to melt.*

Sundried Tomato, Parmesan and Olive-crusted Rack of Lamb with a Warm Green Bean and Pine Nut Salad

Rack of lamb is a very stylish dinner party dish and the Mediterranean flavours I have put into the crust are really delicious.

* serves six
  takes about 50 minutes to make

Preheat the oven to 220°C/fan 200°C/gas 7.

Season the lamb all over with salt and pepper. Heat a trickle of olive oil in a roasting tray or a large ovenproof frying pan over a medium heat. Add the lamb, fat-side down, and fry for 5 to 8 minutes until the fat is melting and becoming golden. Increase the heat and brown all over to seal the meat. Remove the lamb and sit on a board.

To make the crust, mix together the breadcrumbs, oregano or thyme, Parmesan, olives and 3 tablespoons olive oil. Season with salt and pepper.

Spread the sundried tomato paste over the fat side of the racks of lamb, and then press the crust on top.

Scatter the onion wedges in the roasting tray or frying pan and turn in the lamb fat in the bottom. Sit the lamb, crumb-side up, on top. Roast for 20 minutes to cook the lamb to a pinkish finish (cook for longer if you prefer your lamb well done). While the lamb is roasting, cook the beans in boiling salted water for about 5 minutes until just tender. Drain well.

Heat a frying pan with the olive oil and gently cook the pine nuts until they are just golden. Add the garlic and remove from the heat. Toss into the green beans, season with salt and pepper and add the lemon juice.

Remove the cooked lamb from the oven and leave to rest for about 5 minutes. Carve the rested lamb, either slicing each rack in half or into individual cutlets. Serve with the onion wedges and salad.

for the lamb

3 racks of lamb
  (6–8 bones per rack),
  French trimmed
sea salt and freshly
  ground black pepper
olive oil
75g fresh white breadcrumbs
1 heaped tablespoon chopped
  oregano or thyme leaves
75g Parmesan cheese, grated
15 black olives, pitted and
  finely chopped
3 tablespoons sundried
  tomato paste
4 large red onions, peeled
  and cut into wedges

for the salad

600g green beans,
  tops trimmed
4 tablespoons extra-virgin
  olive oil
100g pine nuts
3 cloves of garlic, crushed
sea salt and freshly ground
  black pepper
juice of 1 small lemon

Black Forest Soufflés with Cherry Brandy

The very thought of making a soufflé fills most people with instant fear, but they really aren't that hard to do providing you get a couple of things done ahead. First, prepare the soufflé dishes and sit them in the fridge until needed. Then make the chocolate cream base and set aside. All you need to do at the last minute is whisk the egg whites, mix in the chocolate cream and pour into the dishes. That's it. You now have fifteen minutes to sit back down and enjoy another glass of wine while they cook (or do what I often do, and press your nose up against the oven door in anticipation, watching them rise).

* serves six
takes about 45 minutes to make

First off, prepare six 150ml ramekin dishes for foolproof soufflé rising. Brush the butter all the way round the inside of the dishes, using upward strokes from the bottom of the dishes to the top. Place in the fridge until set.

Brush on another layer of butter using the same action, and then coat with a layer of the grated chocolate. Put a tablespoon of cherries in the bottom of each ramekin and leave in the fridge until you need them.

To make the chocolate cream, place the milk in a non-stick saucepan and heat until almost boiling. Remove from the heat and stir in the chocolate until melted.

Beat together the cornflour, egg yolks and 50g of the caster sugar until smooth. Stir in the chocolate milk, and then return the whole lot to the pan. Place over a gentle heat and stir continuously until thickened and smooth. If it becomes lumpy, just push through a sieve with a rubber spatula to remove the lumps. Stir in the cherry brandy and transfer to a clean bowl. Cover the surface directly with clingfilm to prevent a skin forming and leave to cool at room temperature.

20g unsalted butter, melted and cooled

20g grated dark chocolate

6 tablespoons cherries in syrup or a marinade, drained

250ml milk

150g dark chocolate (70% cocoa solids), broken into small pieces

20g cornflour

3 large eggs, separated

75g caster sugar

50ml cherry brandy

white chocolate shavings or grated white chocolate, to serve

So, that's the hard work done. Now all you need to do is finish them off when you are ready.

Preheat the oven to 200°C/fan 180°C/ gas 6.

Whisk the egg whites in a clean bowl until they form peaks, and then gradually whisk in the remaining 25g of caster sugar until you have firm peaks.

Stir a third of the egg white into the chocolate cream to loosen it, and then gently fold in the rest. Spoon into the prepared ramekins, levelling off the tops with a palette knife to give a super flat surface. Place on a baking tray and bake in the oven for 15 minutes until they have risen and smell wonderfully chocolaty.

The second they come out of the oven, sit the ramekins on plates, scatter over a little white chocolate and serve straight away.

PS... *On each plate, place a Chinese-style spoon with a scoop of ice cream on it next to the soufflé. Get everyone to break a hole in the centre of their soufflé as soon as they get it and drop the ice cream into the middle.*

Seafood Paella

If you fancy a big get-together at your place, a pan of paella is a great choice. Once all the ingredients are prepared, it takes very little effort, and though it's not the cheapest of recipes, it's well worth it when you are in the mood for being extravagant. Try and pick up a large paella pan — they are really cheap, come in all sizes and give a very authentic look to the finished paella.

* serves eight
takes about 45 minutes to make

Heat the olive oil in a paella pan or a very large frying pan. If you haven't one big enough, use two pans or a heavy-bottomed roasting tray. Add the onion and garlic and sauté until the onion has softened.

Stir in the rice for a minute or so until it is coated in the oil, then add the wine, saffron, paprika and enough stock to cover the rice (about two-thirds of the measured quantity). Stir well and bring to a simmer. Allow to gently cook for about 10 minutes, stirring occasionally to prevent the rice sticking to the bottom of the pan. Add some more stock if it is being absorbed too quickly.

Stir in the mussels, clams, peeled prawns, squid, peas and peppers and season with salt and pepper. Arrange the whole prawns on top and pour over the remaining stock. Cover tightly with foil and leave to gently cook over low heat for about 10 to 15 minutes, until the rice is tender and the seafood is cooked through (the mussel and clam shells should be open).

Sprinkle over the parsley and place the lemon wedges on top. Serve the paella straight away, making sure everyone gets a whole prawn and a wedge of lemon.

PS... *To clean the mussels and clams, wash and scrub under cold running water, discarding any open shells that don't close when tapped. Any shells that haven't opened once the paella is cooked, should be discarded.*

3 tablespoons olive oil

2 onions, chopped

3 cloves of garlic, crushed

600g paella rice
(preferably Calasparra rice)

400ml white wine

a large pinch of saffron strands

2 teaspoons smoked Spanish
paprika (standard paprika
can also be used)

2 litres hot fish or chicken stock

500g mussels, cleaned (see PS...)

250g clams, cleaned (see PS...)

250g raw tiger prawns, peeled

4 small squid, cleaned and
cut into rings

200g frozen peas, defrosted

2 roasted red peppers,
cut into strips (ones from
a tin or jar are ideal)

sea salt and freshly ground
black pepper

8 raw tiger prawns, shell on

1 small bunch of flat-leaf
parsley, chopped

8 lemon wedges

Sangria Jellies with Lemon Cream

Follow on with the Spanish theme and offer this as a dessert. Unlike the drink, these softly set jellies won't give you a head-splitting hangover (or is it just me that suffers from killer sangria hangovers?).

* **makes eight**

takes about 15 minutes to make, plus at least 4 hours setting time

Place the red wine in a saucepan and heat until it's almost, but not quite, boiling. Using scissors, cut the orange and lemon jelly into cubes and stir into the red wine until it has totally melted. Leave to cool while you prepare the oranges.

Cut the top and bottom off each orange and sit flat on a board. Following the curve of the orange, cut away the peel and pith using a sharp knife. Hold the orange in your hand over a measuring jug to catch the juices, cut out the segments, and then cut each segment into two. Dry the orange segments on kitchen paper.

Squeeze any juice out of the remaining part of the oranges and then top up with the fresh orange juice to give you about 300ml of juice. Pour it into the cooled wine and jelly mixture.

Divide the orange pieces among eight wine glasses or dishes. Pour over the jelly and chill in the fridge for at least 4 hours, or overnight if you can, until set.

To make the lemon cream, simply whisk all the ingredients together until the cream has thickened to form soft peaks. Start by using 6 tablespoons of the sugar, have a taste, and then add the rest if it needs to be sweeter. Spoon the cream on top of the jellies, serving any extra separately.

for the jellies
**600ml red wine
(for something Spanish, try a nice fruity Rioja)**
125g packet of orange jelly
125g packet of lemon jelly
4 sweet, juicy oranges
200ml fresh orange juice

for the lemon cream
300ml whipping cream
juice of 1 lemon
6–8 tablespoons caster sugar

PS... *You can easily turn these into mulled wine jellies for the winter. Heat the red wine with a stick of cinnamon, 1/2 teaspoon cloves and a good grating of nutmeg. Stir in the jelly and leave for about 30 minutes so the spices infuse into the wine. Strain and continue by adding the orange juice as above. The lemon cream can be served with them or, for a change, swap the lemon juice for orange juice.*

Smoked Salmon, Fennel and Radish Salad with Pernod Dill Cream

This simple yet impressive starter can be made in advance to prevent last minute rushing about. The aniseed flavours from the Pernod and fennel work really well with the rich, smoky taste of the salmon.

* serves four (as a starter)
  takes about 15 minutes to make

Mix together the crème fraîche, dill, lemon zest, lemon juice and Pernod. Season well with salt and keep the dressing in the fridge until needed.

Very thinly slice the fennel and radishes. This can be done using a mandolin if you have one; if not, just slice as thinly as possible with a sharp knife. Arrange on plates, squeezing over a little lemon juice if you're not serving the starter straight away to prevent the fennel discolouring. Place the smoked salmon on top, folding it in waves to give a bit of height to the plate.

When you are ready to serve the starter, drizzle over the dressing or serve it separately for everyone to help themselves. Add a twist of black pepper and serve the salad with the bread.

150ml crème fraîche
1 tablespoon chopped dill
grated zest of 1 lemon
a squeeze of lemon juice
1 tablespoon Pernod
sea salt and freshly
  ground black pepper
1 small fennel bulb
1 bunch of radishes
12–16 slices of smoked salmon
  (depending on their size)
thin slices of rye or
  pumpernickel bread

Slow-roast Ginger and Honey Duck with Spring Onion Mash

This delicious duck does take a while to cook, but you'll end up with crisp, sticky skin and tender meat that melts in the mouth. There is also very little to do once it is in the oven, giving you plenty of time to catch up and be the perfect host. It is amazing how little meat there is on a duck once all of the fat has melted and it is cooked, so I have allowed half a duck per person, giving you fairly generous portions. Along with the mash, my favourite vegetable accompaniment is lightly cooked pak choi, broccoli or green beans, tossed in a little sesame oil and hoisin or oyster sauce.

* serves four
takes 2 hours to roast

Preheat the oven to 180°C/fan 160°C/gas 4.

Lightly score the duck skin four to five times on each breast, making sure you don't cut into the flesh. Rub over the grated ginger, salt and pepper, sit the ducks side by side on a rack in a roasting tray and cook for 30 minutes.

After the first half hour of cooking, remove the duck from the oven and spoon over the honey. Return to the oven for a further 30 minutes, and then remove again. Pour off as much of the fat in the bottom of the tray as possible and baste the duck with the hot sticky honey.

Cook for a further hour, basting every 15 minutes or so with the honey, and removing the excess fat as you go. If the honey seems to be burning on the base of the tray, just add a splash of water to loosen it down slightly. After a total of 2 hours cooking, the sticky honey and ginger duck can be removed from the oven. Transfer on to a board or tray and leave to rest for 15 minutes.

for the duck

2 x 1.25–1.5kg oven-ready ducks

25g peeled and finely grated
   fresh ginger

sea salt

1 teaspoon freshly ground
   white peppercorns

6 heaped tablespoons runny honey

1 tablespoon sesame seeds

(continued on page 240)

Pour out any excess fat from the roasting tray and place over a medium heat. Stir in 100ml water and bring to a simmer, scraping any sticky residue from the bottom. Keep warm.

While the duck is roasting, cook the potatoes in boiling salted water for 20 to 25 minutes until tender.

Just before the potatoes finish cooking, place the cream and spring onions in a small saucepan and bring to the boil. Simmer for a couple of minutes, then stir in the butter.

Drain the potatoes, return to the pan and mash well with a potato masher or ricer or, for a really smooth mash, push through a sieve with a rubber spatula. Beat in the onion-flavoured cream and season with salt.

Toast the sesame seeds by heating a frying pan over a high heat, adding the seeds and tossing around until they are lightly golden. Remove from the pan straight away so they don't continue to colour.

To serve the duck, remove the legs and slice off the breasts, serving one of each to every person. Sit the pieces of duck on plates and scatter over the sesame seeds. Serve with the mash, spooning over the ginger and honey gravy from the pan.

PS . . . *As an alternative to the ginger, the freshly grated zest of two oranges can be added to the pan once the duck is cooked, instead of the water.*

for the mash

1.25–1.5kg floury potatoes, such as such as Maris Piper, King Edward or Desiree, peeled and quartered

200ml single cream or milk

1 bunch of spring onions, thinly sliced

25g butter

sea salt

Strawberry Cheesecake Shortbread

This is really speedy to put together, as well as extremely tasty and very stylish looking.

* **serves four**
  takes 10 to 15 minutes to make

To make the cheesecake cream, place the mascarpone in a bowl and beat with a wooden spoon to soften. Whisk in the double cream, caster sugar and vanilla seeds until it is a thick, dolloping consistency. If it becomes too thick, don't worry, it can just be loosened with a little milk. This cream can be made ahead of time and kept in the fridge until needed.

Sit four of the shortbread biscuits on four plates or shallow dishes and layer up with the strawberries, cheesecake cream and the remaining shortbread. Dust with icing or caster sugar, add a sprig of mint and serve straight away.

100g mascarpone cheese, at room temperature

100ml double cream

25g caster sugar

1 vanilla pod, split and seeds scraped out

8–12 thin shortbread triangles or rounds (bought or home-made)

225g strawberries, stalks removed and halved or quartered if large

icing or caster sugar, for dusting

mint sprigs

PS... *Other soft fruits can also be used such as raspberries, cherries, peaches, nectarines, blueberries or blackberries.*

In the Mood for Being
Romantic

You're in the mood for being romantic. Oh my, what a wonderful mood to be in. The world seems to stop and we become totally selfish, putting all of our thoughts and time into each other and not a lot else (it's a good job we don't feel like it all the time, otherwise nothing would ever get done).

There are all sorts of ways to express romance: flowers, a phone call, a nice text, a note under the pillow, presents — I could go on, but I actually think the phrase, 'the way to a man's heart is through his stomach' (which is equally true for women, in addition to diamonds, shoes and handbags — isn't that right, girls?) is the best way every time. Food and love do go hand in hand — the perfect combination and a marriage made in heaven.

There's something deeply fulfilling about cooking for your loved one — seeing the look of admiration, joy and contentment on their face is amazing and they become putty in your hands. Breakfast in bed is one of my favourite meals to be surprised with — providing it is from Phil (my well-trained husband).

Spending time cooking together can be a wonderfully affectionate thing too. Whether it's midweek, when you can catch up on the day's events, or at the weekend, when you can take your time in the kitchen, cooking together can be really romantic and bizarrely quite seductive. Make the most of the occasion by popping open some Champagne or mixing a rather tasty cocktail together (check out some delicious ones in The Cocktail Hour section on page 204). Light a few candles and set the table so you have that special feeling of being in a nice restaurant, but in the private surroundings of your own home (shame about the washing-up afterwards, can you make that fun and seductive?).

Just what do you cook when you are in the mood for being romantic? Well, I think it all depends on when and why the mood arises. We usually find ourselves in a romantic mood on special occasions such as birthdays and anniversaries. But waking up, all snuggled up to your loved one at the weekend, surely calls for a bit of room service in the form of breakfast (or most likely brunch) in bed. If the sun's shining and you fancy some time alone away from home, then a secluded picnic with home-made goodies to nibble on is great. Maybe you want to spice things up a little at the end of the week by cooking a curry together rather than opting for the usual routine of ordering a takeaway? Then, of course, there are the times when you are feeling rather saucy and those aphrodisiac foods come into play, which enhance your mood further.

If you weren't in the mood for a little romance before you read these recipes, you certainly will be afterwards.

Room Service
Romantic breakfasts in bed

I think it has to be one of the most romantic things — having breakfast or brunch brought to you in bed. You are usually put in the mood for romance as soon as you hear the clinking sounds on the tray as your loved one makes their way into the bedroom.

It goes without saying that you'll find yourself in the mood for being romantic on Valentine's Day, birthdays and special occasions, but of course, romance doesn't just stop there.

Weekends and holidays are the best time to make the most of these recipes, when you can take your time and really set the mood. There's nothing better than having a lie-in, getting all romantic and giving your loved one your undivided attention. Set up a tray with their favourite morning treats: freshly brewed coffee, squeezed juice and if you're feeling really loved up, perhaps a few flowers.

Enjoy the morning together, lingering over some lovingly prepared foods. You could even try leaving your tray outside the door in the hope it gets taken away and washed up!

Soft-boiled Eggs with Sexy Soldiers

Soft-boiled eggs are just delicious, with the runny, gooey yolk dripping off your spoon (should I be writing for Jackie Collins?). To make them more special and sexy, serve with toasted and buttered blinis and wonderfully extravagant caviar.

* serves two
takes about 10 minutes to make

Bring a saucepan of water to a simmer and gently lower the eggs into the pan. From the moment the water returns to a simmer, cook for 3 to 5 minutes (3 minutes for a very soft boiled egg, 5 for a firmer one). If the eggs are straight from the fridge, add about 1 minute to the cooking time.

While the eggs are cooking, lightly toast the blinis, spread with butter, and then cut each into three strips to give you soldiers.

Gently take the eggs out of the pan and put into egg cups. Remove the tops, still with some of the egg white in them, then sit on a little pile of sea salt to stop them wobbling around. Place a small amount of caviar on top of each one.

Tuck in by dunking your soldiers in the yolk, followed by scooping up some caviar.

2–4 large very fresh eggs,
at room temperature
4–6 bought blinis
butter
sea salt
2–3 teaspoons caviar

PS . . . *If caviar isn't your thing, then try these:*

* *Chive and sea salt soldiers. Mix together 1 tablespoon of softened butter with a good pinch of sea salt and a couple of teaspoons of finely chopped chives. Spread on top of toasted white bread and cut into soldiers.*

* *You could also flavour your butter with chopped sun-dried tomatoes, tomato ketchup, chopped fresh red chilli or dried chilli flakes, anchovies or pesto.*

* *For some different soldiers altogether, try lightly cooked asparagus wrapped in smoked salmon, strips of crispy bacon, cooked thin sausages, breadsticks or cheese straws.*

In the mood for a drink? *Bloody Mary (page 248), ruby buck's fizz (page 248), or a freshly squeezed orange juice.*

Surprise between the Sheets

Impress your other half with poached eggs and strips of smoked salmon placed between sheets of lasagne and topped with a blanket of very simple, light hollandaise sauce. This takes a bit of preparation time, but is a perfect rewarding brunch for the appetite you'll have worked up.

✳ serves two
takes about 25 minutes to make

First of all, make the hollandaise and keep warm. Place the egg yolk and lemon juice in a screw-top jar or small bottle and shake really well for about 30 seconds. Meanwhile, gently melt the butter either in the microwave or in a small pan. Leave it to sit briefly, and then pour half into the jar. Shake for a further 30 seconds before adding the remaining butter, trying to leave any of the white, milky residue behind. Shake again until the sauce has thickened to a creamy consistency. You can also make the hollandaise by blending in a blender or small food processor, but for these small quantities, using a jar is easier. Keep the jar close to the hob to retain some warmth.

Cook the lasagne sheets in boiling salted water until al dente.

To poach the eggs, bring a medium-size saucepan of water to a simmer with the vinegar. Break in the eggs and, when the water has returned to a simmer, poach for 3 minutes. Lift out with a slotted spoon and sit on kitchen paper to remove the excess water.

To finish the hollandaise, whisk the egg white until it forms soft peaks, and then pour in the butter mixture, a pinch of salt, a pinch of cayenne pepper and the chopped chives. Fold together until you have a light sauce.

To serve up, sit a sheet of pasta on two plates and top with the poached eggs, sliced smoked salmon and a spoon of hollandaise. Lay the second sheet of pasta over the top and finish with some more hollandaise.

Serve straight away and just watch the look of amazement appear on the face of your other half.

for the lasagne
4 sheets of fresh or dried lasagne
2–4 very fresh large eggs
4 tablespoons white wine vinegar or malt vinegar
4–6 slices of smoked salmon

for the hollandaise
1 large egg, separated
2 teaspoons lemon juice
50g butter
sea salt
cayenne pepper
1 tablespoon chopped chives

PS . . . *For a richer sauce, stir 2 to 3 tablespoons of whipped double cream into the hollandaise instead of the whisked egg white.*

Hot Honey Figs
with Ricotta on Fruit Bread

I think figs, with their velvety skin and soft juicy flesh, are the most sensual of all fruits, and they are even better dripping with honey. Why not share this really yummy brekkie with your loved one.

* serves two
  takes about 10 minutes to make

Melt the butter in a frying pan over a medium-high heat. Cut the figs in half and sit them, cut-side down, in the pan. Fry for a few minutes until they are just beginning to become golden.

Increase the heat and drizzle with the honey and 2 tablespoons of water. Turn over the figs and cook for about 30 seconds, and then take the pan off the heat.

While the figs are cooking, lightly toast the bread. Sit on a plate and put the ricotta and roasted figs on top. Spoon over the hot honey and fig syrup from the pan, and then tuck in.

a small knob of butter

4 ripe figs

**2 tablespoons runny honey
  (a fragrant one like orange
  blossom is really lovely)**

4 thick slices of fruit bread

**2 wedges or spoonfuls of
  ricotta cheese**

PS . . . *If you can't get fresh figs, halved and stoned apricots or plums roasted in the same way are also really gorgeous.*

Walnut bread is a great alternative to fruit bread.

Outdoor Pursuits
Picnics for a little alfresco romance

Take some time out together, pack up a parcel of delicious food and hit the great outdoors. There really is something special about sharing some of your favourite food with your loved one while you're sitting on a rug in the park, on the beach or even in your back garden. There are no distractions from the TV, phone (make sure you switch your mobile off) or unexpected visitors. You somehow feel like you have escaped the rest of the world, time has stopped and it's just the two of you.

Romantic picnics can be as simple as sharing a loaf of fresh crusty bread, some soft ripe cheese, juicy cherries, strawberries and a bottle of wine or Champagne. Or, on the other hand, you could really impress your loved one and have a go at some of these delicious recipes. They're perfect for packing up and transporting to your chosen picnic destination when you're in the mood for a romantic alfresco afternoon.

Don't forget a bottle opener and proper wine glasses for a special finishing touch.

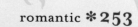

Potted Prawns and Crab with Dill

These little pots of juicy prawns and sweet crabmeat in a delicate, dill-flavoured butter are perfect for a beach picnic. Spread over some rye or crusty brown bread for a light, tasty nibble.

* **makes two**

**takes 10 minutes to make,
plus 45 minutes chilling time**

Gently melt the butter in a saucepan and pour into a jug for all the milky solids to sink to the bottom.

Mix together the prawns, crab, dill and lemon zest and season with salt and a shake of cayenne pepper. Divide between a couple of small pots or ramekins and pack down really well with the back of a spoon.

Pour over the clear (clarified) butter to just cover the mixture, leaving behind the white milky solids. Chill in the fridge for about 45 minutes to set the butter.

Cover each pot with clingfilm and pack in a cool bag with your chosen bread. Don't forget some napkins and a couple of knives to scoop out and spread the potted prawns and crab on to the bread.

75g unsalted butter

100g cooked and peeled small Atlantic prawns

100g white crabmeat (preferably fresh but tinned is fine)

1 teaspoon chopped dill

finely grated zest of ½ lemon

sea salt

cayenne pepper

rye or crusty brown bread

PS . . . *The dill can be replaced with tarragon, chives or basil or to spice the pots up, add ½ a deseeded and finely chopped red chilli.*

In the mood for a drink? *For a light refreshing drink, try an Italian white such as Verdicchio and for a richer, more perfumed option, open a Viognier.*

Salmon and Spring Onion Fritters

These little fritters are perfect for making ahead. Pack into a picnic box and share a pot of sour cream, guacamole and/or sweet chilli dipping sauce to dip them into.

* makes ten fritters
takes about 15 minutes to make

Lightly beat the eggs, and then add the flour and sour cream so you have a thick batter. Stir in the salmon, spring onion and lemon zest and season with salt and pepper.

Heat a tablespoon of olive oil in a frying pan over a low-medium heat. Place tablespoons of the mixture into the pan and press down to form flat fritters. Cook for a couple of minutes until they are golden, and then turn over and cook until the bases are also golden. Repeat with the remaining mixture, adding more oil as you go.

Once the fritters are cool, pack in a box lined with greaseproof paper or a parcel made of greaseproof paper. Don't forget to also pack some sour cream, guacamole and/or a pot of chilli sauce to dip them into.

for the fritters

2 large eggs

100g self-raising flour

4 tablespoons sour cream

200g smoked salmon, cut into strips

4 spring onions, thinly sliced

grated zest of 1 lemon

sea salt and freshly ground black pepper

olive oil

to serve

sour cream

guacamole

sweet chilli dipping sauce

In the mood for a drink? *Go for a zippy light white such as a Sauvignon Blanc or even a Muscadet.*

Cheese and Pickle Pasties

These little pasties are the perfect romantic food for boys. I first made these for my lovely other half, who adores both cheese and pickle sarnies and Cornish pasties for a picnic. I decided to combine the two and ended up with these gorgeous cheese and pickle pasties, gaining loads of brownie points as a result.

* **makes six**
  takes about 25 minutes to make

Preheat the oven to 200°C/fan 180°C/gas 6.

Unroll the pastry and cut into six squares. Spread a heaped teaspoon of pickle in the middle of each one and scatter the cheese on top.

Brush the edges of each pastry square with the egg mixture. Bring to the centre and fold and pinch the pastry together to form a Cornish pasty shape.

Place the pasties on a baking sheet and brush them all over with the egg mixture. Bake for 15 to 18 minutes until they are crispy and golden. Leave to cool slightly and eat them warm or set aside until cold.

375g ready-rolled puff pastry

6 heaped teaspoons Branston pickle

250g mature Cheddar cheese, cut into 1cm pieces

1 egg yolk mixed with 1 tablespoon milk

PS . . . *You don't have to stick to Cheddar and pickle, you can play around with whatever flavours you fancy to fill the pasties. Try:*

* *Mozzarella, cherry tomato and basil.*

* *Blue cheese, walnut and sliced apple.*

* *Brie, ham and onion.*

Smoked Duck, Asparagus and Fig Salad

A very simple and sexy salad to share. Both figs and asparagus are known for their aphrodisiac qualities and taste fantastic with the smoked duck and fruity dressing. This is best eaten somewhere secluded.

* serves two
takes about 15 minutes to make

Cut the top and bottom off the orange and sit flat on a board. Following the curve of the orange, cut away the peel and pith using a sharp knife. Hold the orange in your hand over a measuring jug to catch the juices and cut out the segments. Squeeze any juice out of the remaining part of the orange.

In a screw-top jar, mix together the cranberry sauce, olive oil and 1 tablespoon of the saved orange juice. Season with salt and pepper. This dressing is now ready to pour over the salad just before serving.

Cook the asparagus tips in boiling salted water for 2 to 3 minutes until tender. Drain, hold under running cold water to stop them cooking any more, and then dry on kitchen paper.

Place the asparagus in a container with the duck, figs, watercress and orange segments. The salad can now be kept in the fridge until it is needed.

When you are ready to eat, wherever you are, shake the salad dressing and pour over the salad.

1 orange
1 teaspoon cranberry sauce
1 tablespoon olive oil
sea salt and freshly ground
  black pepper
10–12 asparagus tips
100g smoked duck, sliced
2 ripe figs, cut into wedges
½ a bag of watercress

PS . . . *Smoked duck is available to buy prepacked. If you can't get hold of any, try as an alternative cooked chicken, cured ham or smoked salmon.*

In the mood for a drink? *Pinot Noir is a light red which will match the duck meat and the sharp dressing. You could even serve it chilled. Or perhaps Champagne for a special occasion?*

Strawberries and Cream with a Difference

Whenever you think of having a romantic outdoor picnic with your loved one, strawberries and cream are more often than not one of the first things you think of taking. But how many times do you get there and find some of the strawberries are squashed and leaking juice over everything (who put them in the bottom of the bag?) and the cream has either gone warm or the tub has split? Here's a solution: strawberries and cream made into a rather indulgent smoothie. You'll need a very nice container and you'll have to save the seductive strawberry eating for when you get home.

* serves two
   takes 5 minutes to make

Simply blitz everything together in a blender until completely smooth and pour into a nice glass bottle or Thermos. Place a wine chiller around the bottle, pack in a couple of Champagne glasses and you are ready to go.

200g ripe strawberries
150ml strawberry yoghurt
100ml single cream
a good splash of crème de fraise (strawberry liqueur)

PS . . . *If you can be sure they won't get squashed, save a couple of strawberries for garnishing the glasses.*

Friday Night, Curry Night
Spice up your weekend

OK, so it's Friday night, you've had a busy week and you're relieved it's the weekend. You've got no plans to go out and you fancy a little romance with your other half. The problem is you've got into a habit of chilling out in front of the TV with a takeaway, which you usually overorder, subsequently overeat and fall asleep on the sofa before clearing up (nothing romantic about that).

The solution is to spice things up a bit and make your own Friday night curry. No, it doesn't have to be hard work. Get in, get changed, pour yourselves a drink and catch up on the day while preparing some tasty dishes. Cooking together can be really romantic, especially when it's something you both enjoy making.

Now, you might be thinking that a curry isn't very romantic, but believe me, with the exotic aroma wafting around the kitchen while you're cooking and the spicy flavours tantalizing your taste buds, you will soon notice your heartbeat pumping faster and feeling rather hot under the collar.

Just make sure you don't go and ruin all the fun by eating your delicious meal off a tray in front of the TV. Light a few candles to make the place look all cosy and inviting and open a bottle of nice wine. Yes, wine – just because you are having a curry, it doesn't mean you have to have lager. Check out the wine suggestions with the following recipes, all of which work well with the spiciness of the food.

Spoon out a few fruity chutneys and a yoghurt raita into nice dishes either to share with your curry or to dip into with some poppadoms while you're cooking. If you fancy making your own raita, it's really easy and much tastier than bought ones. I like to mix a small pot of natural yoghurt with a handful of finely chopped mint, quarter of a finely chopped or grated cucumber, a pinch of salt and a squeeze of lemon juice. Not only does it taste great, but it also cools things down if they are getting a little too hot.

Chilli and Garlic Prawns with Mango

Forget the greasy samosas and bhajis, go for a starter that won't make you feel too full before you even get to the curry. Share a plate of these mouthwatering prawns and juicy mango, and eat with your fingers for an even more enjoyable experience.

* serves two

**takes 10 minutes to make,
plus 30 minutes marinating time**

Toss the prawns in the garlic, oil, chilli powder, cumin and a pinch of salt, and leave to marinate for about 30 minutes.

Heat a ridged griddle pan or frying pan until it's piping hot. There is no need to add any oil because there is some in the marinade.

Cook the prawns for 1 to 2 minutes on each side until they become nice and golden.

The mango can be served just as it is with the prawns or you can fry the slices briefly on each side before serving.

Arrange the prawns and mango on a plate to share, squeeze over the lemon juice and scatter over the coriander.

Tuck in using your fingers or a fork.

8 large raw tiger prawns, peeled
1 clove of garlic, crushed
2 tablespoons light olive or
   sunflower oil
2 teaspoons chilli powder
½ teaspoon ground cumin
a pinch of sea salt
1 ripe mango, peeled and sliced
a squeeze of lemon juice
a small handful of
   coriander leaves

In the mood for a drink? *Riesling Spätlese from Germany complements the spice and the fruit of the mango.*

Rogan Josh

Please don't be put off by the number of ingredients; this is really easy (and fairly spicy). Leave plenty of time for it to simmer away while you make yourselves busy in other ways — you've got rice and side dishes to prepare!

* **serves two generously**
  takes about 1 hour to cook

In a food processor, blend together the garlic, onion, ginger, red pepper, chilli flakes, cumin seeds, coriander seeds, paprika and salt to create a paste.

Heat the oil in a saucepan or small casserole dish over a high heat and add the lamb pieces, cinnamon stick and cardamom pods. Quickly fry until the lamb is browned all over. Stir in the paste and cook for about 5 minutes.

Pour in the lager or water and the tomatoes and bring to a simmer. Cover with a lid and cook for 50 minutes to 1 hour, stirring occasionally. Remove the lid and cook for a further 5 to 10 minutes, until the sauce has thickened to your liking. Have a taste and season with extra salt if it is needed.

Serve the rogan josh as it is or garnished with fresh coriander, sliced chilli or flakes of coconut. If you think it will be too hot for one of you, add a spoonful of natural yoghurt or raita to the side.

2 cloves of garlic,
  roughly chopped

1 small onion,
  roughly chopped

2.5cm piece of fresh ginger,
  peeled and roughly chopped

½ red pepper, deseeded
  and roughly chopped

½–1 teaspoon dried
  chilli flakes

1 teaspoon cumin seeds

1 teaspoon coriander seeds

2 teaspoons paprika

a good pinch of sea salt

2 tablespoons vegetable oil

500g boneless shoulder of
  lamb, cut into bite-sized cubes

1 cinnamon stick, snapped
  in half

6 cardamom pods, lightly
  crushed with the back of a spoon

100ml lager or water

3 ripe tomatoes, chopped

PS . . . *It's well worth making double the quantity of the curry and keeping half in the freezer for another night.*

In the mood for a drink? *For a spicy experience, rich red Italian Amarone is the ticket for this dish or try more readily available French country reds such as Fitou and Minervois.*

Aromatic Basmati

Follow this 'absorption' method for cooking basmati and you will have perfect, fluffy rice every time. The rice is cooked in a measured amount of water so that by the time it's ready, all the liquid has been absorbed, meaning there is no draining of gloopy, starchy water required. The spices are optional, but do give a great flavour to complement any curry.

* serves two
  takes 15 minutes to cook

Wash the rice in plenty of cold water by shaking it in a sieve under a cold running tap for a few minutes. This will get rid of any excess starch, which can make the rice stodgy.

Put the rice in a small-medium saucepan. Add 275ml water, a pinch of salt and the spices. Place over a medium heat, bring to the boil and cover immediately with a tight-fitting lid. If the lid isn't very tight, cover the pan with foil before putting on the lid. Turn the heat to low and leave to cook for 10 minutes without lifting the lid at all.

200g basmati rice
a pinch of sea salt
1 stick of cinnamon
6 whole cloves
6 cardamom pods, lightly
  crushed with the back
    of a spoon

After 10 minutes, turn off the heat, but you must keep the lid firmly in place because the rice will carry on cooking. Leave for 5 minutes before removing the lid (though it can stay hot for up to 20 minutes if you leave the lid on).

Fluff up the rice with a fork. All of the water should be completely absorbed and your rice should be wonderfully light and fluffy.

Serve with your curry, either with the spices left in or taken out beforehand.

PS . . . *If you like Thai sticky rice, it can be cooked in the same way (but without the spices) to give you perfect sticky rice. The quantities of rice and water can also be doubled or trebled to serve more people. Keep the cooking times the same, just use a bigger pan.*

Panna Cotta with Rose Syrup

OK, so I know that panna cotta is Italian and not Indian, but this is a delightful way to end your spicy curry night. I have adapted the traditional version by adding natural yoghurt to the cream, which makes it more refreshing after the spices. If you like Turkish delight, then you'll love the rose syrup. If you want to go really overboard, scatter the plate with a few pink rose petals — aah, how romantic.

* serves two

> **takes 10 minutes to make,
> plus at least 2 hours setting time**

Sprinkle the powdered gelatine over 1 tablespoon of water and leave to absorb the water for 5 minutes. Alternatively, if you are using leaf gelatine, soak in a flat dish of cold water for 5 minutes.

Place the cream in a saucepan over a medium heat and stir in the sugar and vanilla seeds. Gently bring to the boil, stirring occasionally. Remove from the heat and stir in the gelatine until it has dissolved (if you are using leaf, squeeze out the excess water first). Stir in the yoghurt and strain into a jug.

Using vegetable oil, very lightly grease two moulds, such as ramekins, tea cups, metal or plastic pudding moulds or even heart-shaped moulds, if you like. Pour in the panna cotta mixture.

Set in the fridge for about 2 hours or overnight (if you can), before turning the set panna cottas out on to two plates. If they won't come very easily, then slide a sharp knife down the side to break the air seal or very briefly dip the moulds into hot water.

Pour over the rose syrup and scatter around the pistachios to serve.

**½ teaspoon powdered gelatine
 or 1 leaf of gelatine**

125ml single cream

25g icing sugar

**1 vanilla pod, split and seeds
 scraped out**

125ml natural set yoghurt

**2 tablespoons rose syrup
 (see PS…)**

**1 tablespoon shelled and
 skinned pistachios, halved**

PS... *You can buy beautiful pink rose syrup in bottles from supermarkets or Italian delis, but it tastes much better when it's home-made. To make, boil together 2 tablespoons of caster sugar and 3 tablespoons of water for 1 minute until slightly syrupy. Add ⅛ to ¼ teaspoon of rose water and just enough (1 or 2 drops) pink or red food colouring to give a light pink colour. Leave to cool.*

Food of Love
Aphrodisiac nibbles

So you're in the mood for some sexy and saucy food to seduce and spoil your lover. Foods with aphrodisiac qualities to excite and delight, enhancing your romantic mood further.

There are many scientific thoughts behind why certain foods are classed as an aphrodisiac, but I think that for most people, some foods have an aphrodisiac effect as a result of a personal experience or memory. Maybe fish, chips and Champagne works for you because it was the first meal you shared together by candlelight in your new home. Or sharing that tub of creamy raspberry ripple ice cream after your first hot date makes it now your own personal aphrodisiac.

Of course, there are those obvious aphrodisiacs that seem to work for most of us: asparagus stems dripping in butter, quivering oysters and sweet, juicy strawberries dipped in cream. Whether it's for scientific reasons or just our naughty imagination playing tricks on us, aphrodisiac foods can be pretty powerful at enhancing your romantic mood.

I can't begin to do recipes for all your personal 'foods of luuurve' – the mind boggles at what they could be, so I thought it best to include some of the well-known favourites. They can be served as extravagant and delicious 'teasers' whenever the mood arises or combined with some of your favourite aphrodisiacs to become part of a romantic meal.

Lock the doors, put your phone on silent, and then all you have left to do is think about how and where you serve it.

Oysters

Well, oysters certainly seem to be considered the ultimate aphrodisiac, whether it's because of their libido-enhancing qualities (due to high levels of zinc) or simply their seductive appearance and texture. So I just had to include them in this section of the book. They're definitely one of my favourite foods of love — so much so that we served them at our wedding reception.

It doesn't matter how many oysters you buy. Six per person is usual, but it's up to you. Just make sure they are superfresh with tight, shut shells.

To Open the Oysters

This isn't the easiest job in the world, but with a bit of practice, you can become an expert. You can ask your fishmonger to do it for you, but for me, opening them yourself is all part of the oyster experience.

Scrub the oysters clean with a brush under the cold tap. Hold an oyster with a cloth or tea towel, flatter-side up. Insert an oyster knife or clean screwdriver into the pointed tip of the oyster (the hinge), push and twist and the oyster will almost pop open. Be patient as some are easier than others. Remove the top shell and gently loosen the oyster so it's unattached within the remaining half.

Place the opened oysters on a platter of crushed ice and enjoy straight away with a squeeze of lemon, twist of pepper or Tabasco sauce. Or try one of the following dressings, served in a small bowl or glass to spoon over your oysters.

PS . . . *You don't have to serve oysters raw — some people are a little squeamish about them. You could always pan-fry your oysters by removing them from their shells and lightly tossing in flour seasoned with cayenne pepper and salt. Sauté in butter and olive oil for about 3 minutes, squeeze over some lemon juice and scatter with parsley or serve with any of the sauces.*

Passion Fruit and Sesame Oysters

Mix everything together and serve alongside the oysters or, if you don't want to keep in the passion fruit pips, strain the juice through a sieve first.

1 passion fruit

2 teaspoons sesame oil

juice and grated zest of ½ lime

a pinch of sea salt

Sweet and Sour Oysters

Mix together and leave to infuse for 30 minutes before serving with the oysters.

¼ red chilli, finely chopped

2 tablespoons rice wine vinegar or white wine vinegar

1 teaspoon caster sugar

½ teaspoon grated fresh ginger

1 teaspoon chopped coriander leaves

Ginger, Wasabi and Soy Oysters

Mix together and serve alongside the oysters.

2 teaspoons finely chopped sushi ginger

2 pea-sized amounts of wasabi paste

2 tablespoons light soy sauce

Chilli Vodka and Tomato Oysters

Mix everything together and serve spooned over the oysters.

1 tablespoon chilli-flavoured vodka

½ teaspoon tomato purée

a pinch of celery salt

a few drops of Worcestershire sauce

a good squeeze of lemon juice

In the mood for a drink? *You're spoilt for choice . . . Champagne, a crisp Prosecco, ice-cold Chablis or Hoegaarden beer are all great with oysters.*

Asparagus with Melting Brie

Not only is asparagus rather seductive to eat, it's also believed to contain properties that alleviate stress — perfect for first-date nerves. Tuck into this whenever the mood arises or serve as a starter.

* serves two
takes 10 minutes to make

Preheat the grill to medium.

Snap the asparagus about 2 to 4cm from the base of the stalks (they should naturally have a breaking point) and trim away any tough-looking pointy 'ears' on the stalks.

Place the spears in a deep frying pan or wide saucepan of boiling salted water. Cook for 2 to 4 minutes, depending on their thickness, until just tender. Remove with a slotted spoon and shake off any excess water.

Place the asparagus in an ovenproof serving dish and roll in the butter and a pinch of salt. Lay the slices of Brie over the top and place under the grill until the Brie has melted and is oozing over the asparagus.

Serve straight away, eating with your fingers with the Brie dripping off each spear.

1 bunch of asparagus

a knob of butter

sea salt

5–6 slices of ripe Brie,
thinly sliced

PS . . . *Creamy Camembert is also very tasty on top of the asparagus.*

In the mood for a drink? *Asparagus is a sensation with Sauvignon Blanc, with its pungent herby character or try a steely style Chardonnay from Chablis.*

Prawn and Avocado Champagne Tempura

Traditional Japanese tempura batter is wonderfully light, crisp and really easy to make because there are very few ingredients and hardly any mixing required. This recipe gives you an even more delicate batter from using Champagne (or sparkling wine). This is the perfect finger food to tease each other with for a starter, snack or a light main course, especially when dipped in sweet chilli sauce to spice things up a little.

* serves two
takes about 15 minutes to make

Pour enough oil into a wok, large pan or deep-fat fryer to come halfway up the pan. If you have a thermometer, heat to 180°C. If not, check the oil is at the right temperature by dropping in a 2 to 3cm cube of bread. It should be golden and crisp in just 1 minute.

Place the flour, cornflour and salt in a bowl and mix in the Champagne with a chopstick or the handle of a wooden spoon until it is just combined. The mixture should be thin and slightly lumpy, which will give you a lovely crisp batter.

When the oil is ready, dust the prawns and avocado in the 3 tablespoons of flour, and then briefly dip into the batter. Drop straight into the oil, a few at a time, for just 1 to 2 minutes until pale golden and crisp.

Drain on kitchen paper and serve straight away with a dish of chilli sauce to dip into.

sunflower or vegetable oil,
   for deep-frying
50g plain flour, plus
   3 tablespoons extra
   for dusting
1 teaspoon cornflour
a pinch of sea salt
100ml chilled Champagne
   or sparkling wine
8 large raw prawns, peeled
   but tails left on if possible
1 small avocado, sliced
sweet chilli dipping sauce,
   to serve

PS . . . *If you can't bring yourself to use Champagne or sparkling wine in the tempura batter (surely you'll be opening a bottle anyway?), then it can be made in the same way but using chilled sparkling water.*

Asparagus or red peppers can be used in addition to prawns and avocado.

Buttered Truffle Spaghetti

This is delicious with the musky flavour and aroma of truffle. Now, I am not suggesting you hunt high and low for fresh truffles (not to mention having to take out a bank loan to buy them), instead you can buy great truffle oils that add an amazing flavour to the pasta. You'll only want a small bowl each though unless you're sharing. Too much pasta can be filling and makes you sleepy — not what you intend happening, I am sure.

* serves two

**takes up to 15 minutes to make,
depending on the spaghetti you use**

Cook the spaghetti until al dente. Drain, reserving about 2 tablespoons of the cooking water in the pan. This helps to create a creamy sauce.

Return the pasta to the reserved water in the pan and add the butter and half of the Parmesan. Stir over a low heat until a cheesy, buttery sauce clings to the pasta.

Stir in the truffle oil, a teaspoon at a time, until you have the desired flavour. Truffle oils vary in strength depending on the brand, so taste the pasta as you go to avoid adding too much.

Season with a pinch of salt and a good twist of black pepper. Serve in two small bowls or one large bowl to share, with the remaining Parmesan scattered over the top.

150g spaghetti

50g butter

50g Parmesan cheese, finely grated

truffle oil

sea salt and freshly ground black pepper

PS . . . *Have a look out in your local supermarket or deli for jars or bottles of preserved truffles. They can be thinly shaved into the pasta as an alternative, or an addition, to the truffle oil. Truffle paste is also worth searching out to add to the pasta. If you are lucky enough to get a fresh truffle, then you really are being decadent! It just needs to be shaved into the pasta once cooked.*

In the mood for a drink? *Rich white Chardonnay from Burgundy is sublime.*

Pan-fried Strawberries in Vanilla Thyme Syrup

I don't know if it's the heart shape of strawberries or their soft, juicy flesh that makes us regard them as a sexy food, but whatever it is, rather than serving them alone, with cream or dipped in chocolate, why not be different and create this impressive recipe in no time at all. Not only does it taste great, but the vanilla is believed to increase lust and thyme was once thought to stimulate amorous instincts. You could well be in for an interesting time after eating this.

* **serves two**
  takes about 10 minutes to make

Heat a frying pan over a high heat and add the butter. Once it is bubbling, add the strawberries and cook for just 2 to 3 minutes, turning occasionally until they are just beginning to soften.

Remove the strawberries, leaving 8 to 10 halves behind, and spoon into dishes.

Lightly squash the remaining strawberries in the pan and scrape in the vanilla seeds. Add the thyme sprig, sugar and 3 tablespoons of water and bring to the boil. Cook for about 2 minutes, and then strain through a sieve over the strawberries. Finish with a twist of black pepper to add a little kick and a tingle to your lips.

a knob of unsalted butter

400g ripe strawberries, halved if large

1 vanilla pod

1 small sprig of thyme

3 tablespoons caster sugar

freshly ground black pepper

PS . . . *A scoop of good vanilla ice cream or clotted cream and a crispy shortbread biscuit are very nice accompaniments if you are feeling a little more indulgent.*

Exotic Chocolate Cups

Chocolate is a well-known aphrodisiac. It's said to contain natural substances that increase sexual appetite and act as a stimulant to both the body and the mind. Whether it's true or not, these silky smooth, exceptionally rich chocolate desserts served in small coffee cups are a real treat. The exotic hint of allspice and rum will certainly get your taste buds excited.

* serves two

takes about 10 minutes to make, plus a few hours chilling time

Heat the cream, orange zest, sugar and allspice in a small pan until the cream is just bubbling, but not quite boiling. Remove from the heat and drop in the chocolate, stirring until it is melted.

Beat in the egg yolk, rum and butter until smooth.

Pour into two espresso cups and leave to set in the fridge for a few hours.

The cups can be eaten straight from the fridge or, for a softer consistency, left at room temperature for about an hour first. Serve the cups on saucers or a platter, with a teaspoon or little crispy biscuits on the side to scoop up the rich chocolate.

75ml single cream

zest of 1 small orange

1 tablespoon caster sugar

a small pinch of ground allspice

50g dark chocolate (70% cocoa solids), chopped

1 large egg yolk

1 tablespoon dark rum

10g unsalted butter, softened

PS... *You can lighten up these chocolate cups to create a mousse-like consistency by folding in a whisked egg white to the warm chocolate mixture, and then pouring into coffee cups rather than espresso cups. Rather than using dark rum, try Malibu for a subtle coconut flavour.*

Index

Thank you, thank you, thank you...

I would like to say a huge thanks to all the people who have helped make this book possible.

Firstly – Phil (aka The best-fed man in London), my fab husband. Thanks a million for your incredible support and encouragement in everything I do, and especially for this book. Sorry for all the late nights at the computer and the chaos I caused in the kitchen... on a daily basis. You have the patience of a saint!

Big hugs to both my grandmas and my mum for introducing me to such great food when I was growing up, and for the fun we had in the kitchen.

Thanks to all my brilliant friends and family for being such great guinea pigs when the recipes were in their development stages – sorry for any expanded waistlines!

A massive thanks to the amazing Camilla Stoddart at Penguin for believing in the idea for this book from the beginning and for her endless enthusiasm throughout. I would like to thank everyone else at Penguin, especially the lovely Sarah Fraser for designing this book so beautifully and being my fellow model. Anwen Hoosen, Yeti McCaldin for the stunning illustrations, Georgina Atsiaris, Sarah Hulbert, Helen Reynolds, Belinda Rapley and Karol Davies, the wonderful sales team and of course the enthusiastic recipe testers. Thanks also to Kay Halsey for her fabulous editing.

A huge round of applause to the talented Olly Smith (www.ollysmith.com) for the brilliant wine matches to many of these recipes. Subscribe to his free monthly wine email bulletin subscribe@hotbottle.co.uk for up-to-date booze recommendations.

I think the photography in this book looks fabulous – so a huge thanks to Gus Filgate for the beautiful shots (and to Chris Terry for the stunning jacket), and to Tom Rowlandson (kitchen slave boy!) for all his hard work and assistance in preparing the food for the shots.

A special thanks to Gary Rhodes, whom I have learnt so much from working with over the years. Sorry I didn't ask you to assist me on the photoshoot!

Thanks to Martine Carter at DML, my lovely agent.

Finally, a great big thanks to everyone who buys this book. I hope you enjoy using it as much as I enjoyed putting it together.